Crimesploitation

The Cultural Lives of Law
Edited by Austin Sarat

Crimesploitation

Crime, Punishment, and Pleasure on Reality Television

Paul Kaplan and Daniel LaChance

Stanford University Press

Stanford, California

Stanford University Press
Stanford, California

Printed in the United States of America on acid-free, archival-quality paper

Library of Congress Cataloging-in-Publication Data

Names: Kaplan, Paul, 1968– author. | LaChance, Daniel, 1979– author.
Title: Crimesploitation : crime, punishment, and pleasure on reality
    television / Paul Kaplan and Daniel LaChance.
Other titles: Cultural lives of law.
Description: Stanford, California : Stanford University Press, 2022. |
    Series: The cultural lives of law | Includes bibliographical references
    and index.
Identifiers: LCCN 2021062079 (print) | LCCN 2021062080 (ebook) | ISBN
    9781503613683 (cloth) | ISBN 9781503631731 (paperback) | ISBN
    9781503631748 (ebook)
Subjects: LCSH: True crime television programs—United States—History and
    criticism. | Reality television programs—United States—History and
    criticism. | Crime on television. | Punishment on television.
Classification: LCC PN1992.8.T78 K37 2022 (print) | LCC PN1992.8.T78
    (ebook) | DDC 791.45/6556—dc23 /eng20220302
LC record available at https://lccn.loc.gov/2021062079
LC ebook record available at https://lccn.loc.gov/2021062080

Cover design: Michel Vrana
Cover photos: iStock

For our mentors:
Elaine Tyler May, Lary May, and Austin Sarat (DL)
Kitty Calavita, Simon Cole, Valerie Jenness, and Richard Leo (PK)

Contents

Acknowledgments

It takes a village to "raise" a book, and we are grateful for the feedback of colleagues who offered feedback and advice on this project at various stages: Michelle Brown, Hank Fradella, Stuart Henry, Caley Horan, Alex Milla, Ryan Murphy, Keramet Reiter, Alessandra Rellini, and Colin Reynolds. Particular thanks go to Renée Cramer and Ashley Rubin, who read and commented on multiple drafts of the manuscript. Michelle Lipinski's editorial enthusiasm for this project in its earliest stages convinced us to turn it into a book and submit it to the "Cultural Lives of the Law" series at Stanford University Press. We are grateful for the support of the press and, in particular, Sunna Juhn and Marcela Maxfield. Emory undergraduate students Sueda Polat and Jenna Yun provided exceptional research assistance. Finally, we appreciate the ongoing intellectual and logistical support we receive from our colleagues in the School of Public Affairs at San Diego State University and the Department of History at Emory University.

Parts of the introduction and chapters 2 and 4 have been published elsewhere in different forms. Some of the material on *To Catch a Predator* appeared in *Law, Culture, and Humanities* 15, no. 1 (2019): 127–50. Some of the material on *Making a Murderer* appeared in *Crime, Media, Culture* 16, no. 1 (2020): 81–96. We introduced crimesploitation as a term in contributions to *The Oxford Research Encyclopedia of Criminology and Criminal Justice* (2017) and *The Routledge International Handbook of Visual Criminology* (2017).

Our work has benefited from feedback we received from colleagues at the Annual Meetings of the American Criminology Society, the Association for the Study of Law, Culture, and the Humanities, the Law and

Society Association, and the Western Society for Criminology. Finally, this work benefited from financial support given by Emory University College of Arts and Sciences and the Princeton University Program in Law and Public Affairs.

Our friends and family sustained us through the years we've worked on this project. Daniel thanks Dana Bontemps, Joey Brakefield, Rachel Buchberger, Nick Eigen, Nihad Farooq, Andy Grover, Jeff Hnilicka, Karen and John LaChance, Amanda Mahnke, Todd Michney, Melissa Miness, Annie Murray-Close, Zak Taylor, Dan Weiner, and Ali John Zarrabi. Paul thanks Peter M. Blair, Dimitri A. Bogazianso, Brian Goeltzenleuchter, Peri Good, Valerie Hastie, David Jancsics, Jasper Kaplan, Jeffrey P. Kaplan, Julie O'Connor-Quinn, Charlie Pizarro, SMART and We Agnostics Buddies, and Sylvia Valenzuela.

Crimesploitation

Introduction

The Disciplined and the Delinquent

When the television show *Cops* celebrated its five-hundredth episode in 2002, reporters asked its creator to reflect on the show's success. John Langley, who left a career as a philosopher to develop the show, explained that network executives initially balked at what he pitched to them. A show with no host or narrator, comprised solely of footage shot by camera operators shadowing actual police officers? Audiences would not know what to make of it. And police agencies—notoriously insular organizations—would never subject themselves to such scrutiny. Nonetheless, the fledgling Fox Television Network decided to take a risk. The show became an immediate hit. Airing "the dirty laundry of society," as Langley put it, *Cops* drew up to 11 million viewers a week, including celebrity fans like Sylvester Stallone and Cher.[1]

When it premiered in 1989, *Cops* marked the dawn of a new age of "reality television"—unscripted, formulaic programs that portray people acting as themselves—doing their jobs, vying in weeks-long competitions, or simply living and socializing with one another.[2] By the early twenty-first century, *Cops* was competing with dozens of reality television shows that promised audiences unfiltered access to scenes of crime and punishment, from novice police officers chasing burglary suspects through backyards to middle-aged men planning sexual liaisons with underage adolescents to drug-addicted mothers fleeing bounty hunters.[3] Contemplating the remarkable success of *Cops*, Langley pointed to something profound beneath the "head-cracking, obscenity-laced melees" he aired on American television screens.[4] *Cops*, he told an interviewer, was an "existential variety show with authentic décor."[5]

This book takes Langley's off-the-cuff musing seriously. Evoking the works of Fyodor Dostoyevsky, Simone de Beauvoir, and Jean-Paul Sartre, *existential* is not a word typically associated with reality television. *Trashy* more readily comes to mind. But as we hope to show, existential anxiety drives *Cops* and the many crimesploitation programs that followed in its footsteps. In the chapters that follow, we argue that these shows served as a window into the different, sometimes contradictory experience of life in a world that had undergone—and continues to undergo—massive social and economic changes. Those changes made many Americans feel culturally and financially insecure. These programs offered them different ways of understanding and managing that insecurity.

The Cultural Road to Crimesploitation

We call the reality television programs that are the focus of this book "crimesploitation" because they blend key elements of two long-standing genres: "true crime" texts, which dramatize actual criminal cases investigated and prosecuted by authorities, and "exploitation" films, which satisfy the voyeuristic desire to witness the violation of taboos.[6]

Broadly defined, "true crime" refers to texts that turn actual crimes, criminal trials, or punishments into stories that are consumed by a wide public. Such texts can run the gamut from highbrow fare that aims to make lasting aesthetic and thematic contributions to American letters to formulaic, lowbrow productions that aim to entertain mass audiences. They often share a common thread. In them, criminality "appears both as very close and quite alien, a perpetual threat to everyday life, but extremely distant in its origin and motives, both everyday and exotic in the milieu in which it takes place."[7] The earliest true crime took the form of accounts of crimes and executions that circulated in pamphlet form as early as the sixteenth century in Europe.[8] Americans have, as we might expect, long consumed these texts. One of the earliest "bestsellers" in colonial North America was Mary Rowlandson's salacious 1682 account of her experience in captivity at the hands of Native Americans.[9] Eighteenth- and nineteenth-century Americans could find written accounts of crime and punishment in widely circulating print materials. Eighteenth-century broadsides—cheap mass-produced documents—chronicled the crimes and executions of murderers. Nineteenth-century theaters performed plays based on actual murder cases. When a Methodist minister was put on trial for the 1832 murder of factory worker Sarah Maria Cornell in Fall River, Massachusetts, accounts of the crime and its aftermath became the source for no fewer than three different plays.[10] Starting in the mid-nineteenth century, tabloid-style newspapers melodramatically covered sensational criminal trials that periodically gripped a city's or the nation's imagination.[11]

With the introduction of new entertainment technologies, true crime proliferated in new forms. Radio programs of the 1930s like *True Detective Mysteries, Homicide Squad, Calling All Cars*, and *Treasury Agent* turned actual police files into radio dramas. Big-screen police procedurals in the 1940s were often fictionalized versions of cases investigated by the Federal Bureau of Investigation (FBI) and local police agencies. Filmed on location, they sought to convey a sense of "reality" by adopting a "documentary look—a gritty realism."[12] By the late 1960s one of the most popular shows on television was *The FBI*. Forty million Americans a week tuned into ABC to watch a show about a group of heroic, fictional FBI agents solving crimes inspired by actual FBI cases.

Over time, law enforcement increasingly perceived benefits in collaborating with the creators of true crime texts. FBI director J. Edgar Hoover served as a consultant for *The FBI*, turning to the media to burnish his agency's public image. In exchange for his cooperation, the show's producers ceded editorial control to Hoover and his second-in-command, Clyde Tolson, who vetted scripts and declared some material off limits.[13] Authorities also sought to transform true crime productions into opportunities to expand their surveillance powers. *The FBI* often ended with a segment that introduced audiences to a fugitive and asked them to contact the authorities. In the 1970s authorities' efforts to capitalize on the popularity of true crime stories took a turn toward the local, as regional news stations and police departments worked together to produce "crimestoppers," segments that reenacted unsolved crimes and then solicited viewers' help in bringing the perpetrators to justice. When the first contemporary crimesploitation shows emerged in the late 1980s, two of them, *Unsolved Mysteries* (1987) and *America's Most Wanted* (1988), revived a well-established tradition of entertaining audiences with stories of crime and then asking for their assistance in capturing the culprits.[14]

If crimesploitation reflects true crime's longstanding preoccupation with criminal justice, its quasi-pornographic qualities mark its connection to twentieth-century exploitation films. From 1920 to 1960 enterprising filmmakers made countless cheap films aimed at satisfying audiences' desire for knowledge about off-limits topics. Cultural historian Eric Schaefer identifies several key features of these films. First, they focused on forbidden topics, like sexual promiscuity or illicit drug use, promising viewers "shocking truths and fearless frankness." Second, they often displaced taboo desires onto exotic "others," people who seemed racially, sexually, and morally foreign to middle-class audiences. One iteration of the genre took viewers on journeys into dangerous jungles in far-flung locales where they could encounter topless "native girls" (California actors), gorillas (men in ape suits), and scenes of cannibalism (faked). Finally, while their goal was to titillate, exploitation films pretended to have a pedagogical purpose, presenting themselves as warnings about threats to middle-class decency. "Square-ups," statements about "the social or moral ill the film claimed to combat," would appear before a film began, offering a respectable reason to watch the film. For example, after Congress passed the Harrison Narcotic Act (1914), which banned opium and cocaine at the national level, a slew of exploitation films presented themselves as cautionary tales, depicting "middle- or upper- class individuals abusing a variety of substances and eventually becoming derelicts."[15]

The classical era eventually gave way to fictional exploitation films that were less concerned with maintaining a veneer of respectability. Indeed, they advertised themselves as offering thrills that audiences would not find elsewhere. As film scholar Calum Waddell notes, modern exploitation films "capitalized on social anxieties of the 1960s and 1970s" by depicting "facets of contemporary socio-political 'taboo': interracial sex, the insatiable female, a verité approach to torture and murder, African-American hypersexuality and revolt." It was in this era that media critics devised a versatile way to describe these sorts of texts, making a portmanteau out of the word *exploitation* and the taboo object or scenario that was being exploited for mass consumption. The NAACP coined the term "Blaxploitation" to condemn exploitation films in the 1970s that, they charged, glorified "black males as pimps, dope pushers, gangsters and super males with vast physical prowess but not cognitive skills."[16] Other 'sploitations, like "sexploitation," followed.[17]

Ideologically and aesthetically, the shows we study borrow much from exploitation films. Just as classical exploitation films offered audiences access to underworlds they would not normally encounter, crimesploitation offers audiences the opportunity to consume what they have been told is off limits. If "junkies," "primitive" peoples, and female sex workers—prostitutes, strippers, burlesque women—populated classical exploitation, contemporary crimesploitation offers its own kaleidoscopic array of deviants, from "hookers" to "gang-bangers" to child molesters, who inspire both curiosity and revulsion. Episodes of *Intervention* offer close-up views of crack smoking. *Bait Car* regales viewers with the highs and lows of stealing a car and getting arrested for it. *Lockup* takes viewers into the bowels of maximum-security prisons. Other shows depict ordinary-seeming people engaging in forbidden behavior. A ride-along policing show, *Alaska State Troopers*, shows intoxicated snowmobile drivers stopped for drunk driving. And, like both classical and late twentieth-century exploitation films, these shows aim to create a sense of "gritty verisimilitude" for their viewers.[18] The shaky movements of hand-held cameras, the grainy texture of surveillance footage, and uncomfortable close-ups all convey a sense of "documentary immediacy" that late twentieth-century exploitation films pioneered.[19]

While crimesploitation evolved out of long-standing elements of true crime and exploitation texts, it was also the product of a world in which it had become easier than ever to deliver "gritty verisimilitude" to audiences. As Mark Fishman and Gray Cavender note, new recording technologies like closed-circuit television surveillance cameras gave producers access to audio and visual recordings that their predecessors could only have dreamed of.[20] The gritty aesthetic that directors of true-crime movies sought to create by filming on location in the 1940s was now easily found in the home movies, security footage, and answering-machine recordings that producers could splice into these shows. Ride-along shows like *Cops* and *Real Stories of the Highway Patrol* were made possible by new production equipment like lightweight cameras and small lavalier microphones that allowed camera operators and participants in reality television programs the ability to work in police cruisers and run after police officers chasing suspects over fences and through backyards.[21] Finally, new transmission and dissemination technologies, such as satellite networks and cable television channels, made it fast and easy for crimesploitation to be produced, transmitted, and consumed.[22]

The Rise of the Neoliberal Carceral State

While crimesploitation drew from long-standing genres, it is best understood as a product of two historical developments in the late twentieth century: the rise of "law and order" politics and the neoliberal transformation of the American economy. Over the course of the 1960s and 1970s conservatives associated a surge in violent crime with the social change that was transforming the nation during these years. In those decades, women, racial minorities, sexual minorities, and youth joined political movements aimed at ending their political and cultural subordination in American society. Within the span of a decade, activists had dismantled a legal regime of racial apartheid, loosened racist immigration laws, gained protections for women against employment discrimination, pressured the medical community to declassify homosexuality as a mental illness, and lowered the voting age to eighteen. To conservatives unsettled by social change, it was no coincidence that it was accompanied by a rise in violent crime. Crime was the consequence Americans were facing for abandoning a way of life that, in their minds, had preserved order in the United States. Nowhere was this association between crime and social change more evident than in the movement for racial equality. As cities burned during uprisings in the summers of the late 1960s, Black liberation became synonymous with Black crime for many white Americans. With the rallying cry of "law and order," politicians called for a repressive state response to crime. "Order," Richard Nixon proclaimed in a campaign ad in 1968, was Americans' "first civil right."[23] Many Americans agreed. With fear of violent crime on the rise, a more punitive approach to the crime problem began to take hold. Fighting poverty, lowering unemployment, and expanding economic opportunities were out. Surveillance, stop-and-frisk, and long prison sentences were in.

The results of this new "law and order" strategy were stupendous and, as we will see, represented a counterrevolution against the social changes of the late 1960s and early 1970s. From the mid-1970s to the late 1980s, the American prison population tripled to about 600,000 people. It would go on to expand massively over the course of the 1990s, doubling again to 1.2 million. By the late 2000s 800 per 100,000 Americans were incarcerated on any given day in the United States—a full 1 percent of the adult population.[24] Many more found themselves navigating a labyrinthine network of institutions designed to manage people on probation, parole, or other forms of noncustodial supervision.

The punitive shift in crime policy was accompanied by an equally dramatic revolution in economic policy. As fear of crime increasingly gripped the nation in the 1970s, the economy began to fail. Economic growth shrank, while inflation skyrocketed—a development that puzzled economists. Since the New Deal influential policymakers had held that the appropriate response to economic decline was the maintenance of a strong regulatory state and the willingness of government to engage in deficit spending to put more money in the pockets of consumers and stimulate economic growth.[25] But such policies seemed to be failing, and elites embraced a more libertarian approach to the economy, one that deregulated enterprise, cut corporate and individual taxes, privatized the provision of many public services, and shrank welfare spending. This approach, known as "neoliberalism," espoused a faith in free markets. Coalescing under Ronald Reagan, neoliberal policies effectively shifted—rather than eradicated—the insecurity created by the economic crises of the 1970s. Tax rates on corporations and the wealthy plummeted, and the nation's gross domestic product began growing again, enriching those at the top of the economic spectrum.[26] But their prosperity did not trickle down to those in lower income brackets, as neoliberal economists suggested it might. By the late 1980s, when the first crimesploitation shows began airing, Americans without a college degree had seen their real wages (the amount of money they earned per hour, adjusted for inflation) decline significantly since the 1970s. Nonunion work in the service industries grew while high-paying unionized jobs declined in response to automation and offshoring of manufacturing.[27] For those who had stepped into the middle classes during the middle decades of the twentieth century—disproportionately white, working-class men and women—the future did not seem as economically secure for their children as it once did. And for those who had hoped to follow in their footsteps, a middle-class existence increasingly seemed out of reach.

Like earlier forms of capitalism, neoliberalism was shaped by racial hierarchies and worked to undermine Black progress in ways that had both economic and carceral consequences.[28] Concerted efforts to remedy Black economic inequality, most notably Lyndon B. Johnson's "Great Society" programs in the 1960s, had sought to offer some assistance to a population that had historically been unable to benefit from welfare programs like the Homestead Act, the Social Security Act, and the G.I. Bill.[29] But when the nation fell into economic crisis in the 1970s, and high inflation and economic stagnation brought decades of prosperity to a screeching halt, the neoliberal policy solutions that politicians embraced had devastating effects on Black Americans. In the name of curbing inflation and jumpstarting the economy, austerity measures slashed the budgets of social spending programs aimed at improving their health, education, and economic security. In an increasingly "sink or swim" economy, many African Americans were relegated to low-paying service industry jobs or, worse, deemed "surplus," neither essential to the growth of the economy nor vested with the potential to become valued participants in it.[30]

With its rejection of structural explanations for social problems, moreover, neoliberalism justified punitive responses to crime that fell hardest on Black people. Idled or disillusioned by an economy that made their economic advancement so improbable, and already "presumed criminal," as historian Carl Suddler has put it, young African American men were conceived as a threat to order. Associated with crime, dysfunction, and decay, Black communities were heavily surveilled and policed. And when police disproportionately detected crime in these communities, neoliberal philosophy primed the punitive cultural response that resulted: a tendency to blame individual immorality, rather than economic and cultural deprivation, for the problem.[31] To those persuaded by the politics of personal responsibility, punishment, not social change, seemed the appropriate response to crime. By now the racial consequences of this thinking are well known. The dramatic rise in incarceration rates for Black men and women became so pronounced that it seemed akin, to some scholars, as a revival of Jim Crow segregation laws in colorblind, carceral form.[32]

It was no coincidence that as markets got "freer," prisons got fuller. American Studies scholar Stephen Dillon argues that neoliberal thought underlay not only elites' response to economic crisis, but also their punitive response to rising crime and social disorder. Studying the mid-twentieth-century writing of neoliberal thinkers Milton Friedman and Friedrich von Hayek, Dillon has argued that neoliberals had long held that the repressive force of the state played a fundamental role in maintaining the order necessary for free markets to function. As Dillon puts it, "In the earliest articulations of what law and order and neoliberalism would be—before a wave of new laws and policy changes took hold in the 1980s—neoliberalism was imagined as a carceral project, and law and order as a neoliberal project."[33] Throughout this book, we call government that embraced free markets while simultaneously caging unprecedented numbers of people the "neoliberal carceral state."

The neoliberal carceral state was something of a paradox. On the one hand, it celebrated individual freedom as a paramount value and deemed government a threat to that freedom. Its antiregulation rhetoric justified cuts to taxes and the welfare services that they supported. On the other hand, government did not shrink. Welfare infrastructure was replaced with penal infrastructure—buildings and bureaucracies dedicated to surveilling, policing, and caging Americans. With those opposed to big government in power, the state began locking up unprecedented numbers of people under the premise that the freedom of responsible citizens depended on the state's capacity to neutralize its irresponsible and dangerous citizens.

It was in this racially charged climate of "libertarianism for the virtuous, and authoritarianism for the vicious" that crimesploitation programs began flourishing in the late 1980s. Treating these programs as cultural artifacts, we argue that they reveal much about the way Americans responded to the rise of the neoliberal carceral state. In the chapters that follow, we advance two central arguments about the cultural work these texts do. The first is that these texts invite viewers to think about criminals and authorities in ways that reinforce the new, neoliberal status quo that emerged in the late twentieth century. The second is that these texts offered audiences varied ways to vicariously experience several different kinds of freedom in an age of growing inequality and punitiveness. At times, crimesploitation offered viewers the vicarious experience of freedom by inviting them to identify with agents of the neoliberal carceral state—police officers, bounty hunters, prosecutors, judges. At other times, the freedom crimesploitation offered was subversive. Sometimes reading against the grain of these texts, we argue that they also enabled opportunities for viewers to find freedom by momentarily identifying with criminals. Such moments offered momentary relief from free markets and the disciplined docility they demanded of good workers and consumers. And they offered satisfying moments of resistance to the coercions of the carceral state and the modern world in which it flourished.

Reinforcing the Neoliberal Carceral State

Crimesploitation, we will show, has worked to reinforce the neoliberal carceral state by telling stories that advance three assumptions. First, crime is the product of intractable cultural or individual pathology. Second, crime is not the product of the unequal distribution of economic, political, and cultural power across a population. Third, the state can contain and harshly punish crime, but it cannot prevent it. By shoring up those assumptions, crimesploitation has attempted to legitimize the broader project of the neoliberal carceral state: the contraction of the state's responsibility for the health and well-being of its citizens and the expansion of its capacity to surveil, police, and punish delinquent or dangerous people.

Crimesploitation reinforces these premises not only through the content of the stories it tells, but also through the format it frequently uses to tell those stories: short, successive segments featuring an endless stream of criminals acting badly. This format distinguishes crimesploitation from fictional accounts of crime. As American Studies scholar Elayne Rapping has noted, fictional crime dramas often embed the cop and the criminal in a longer story that begins before the commission of the criminal deed, giving windows into the sociological and psychological forces that shape the criminal's behavior and the cop's response to it. Not so with most crimesploitation, which never lingers too long on the story of any one criminal or officer. In lieu of "the orderly plot structure of conflict, crisis, and resolution, we have a series of endless, irrational 'disruptions.'"[34] In segment after segment, crimesploitation shows drop the audience into the midst of disorder or potential disorder—a drunken brawl, a vehicle not pulling over, a man sending illicit chat messages to an undercover vigilante. The result is that most of the criminals on crimesploitation programs appear to have no past; for the viewer they exist solely (and forever) in a moment of degradation—out of control, inebriated, high, dissembling, impervious to reason. Crime is not, as religious traditions and tragedies have long suggested, a sinful expression of a flawed and potentially redeemable humanity.[35] These programs teach viewers that crime occurs because criminals are fundamentally different. They are not a product of a social ecosystem that "we" all maintain; they are instead external threats to it.[36] As a result, the criminal justice system is purely reactive. It plays no role in generating the social problems it purports to control.

In the "reality" these shows depict, it becomes hard to imagine different ways of responding to disorder without police and prisons. Since criminal behavior is caused by broken individuals, rather than broken systems, these shows suggest, our options are limited. The best we can do is keep our guard up and be grateful for agents of the law who are doing their best to contain the problem.[37] Indeed, these shows foster a certain kind of "looking" from viewers that does not implicate us in what we see. As critical criminologist Michelle Brown explains, "This kind of looking is fundamentally voyeuristic, distracting, and yet authoritative, inhibiting a deeper interrogation" of that which we consume.[38] For those invested in efforts to radically change the way Americans think about policing and punishment, this type of passivity is particularly invidious when it is encouraged by reality television programs. Studies show that this sort of programming exerts more influence on viewers' attitudes about crime and punishment than fictional works do.[39]

The Peril of Too Much Order

While crimesploitation works to promote viewers' embrace of the neoliberal carceral state, it also enables other viewer experiences. As students of popular culture know, people respond to cultural productions in unpredictable ways and call into question scholars' claims about their supposed ideological effects. Television audiences regularly overlook elements of a story that do not fit their worldview and instead glom onto the parts that do.[40] Moviegoers shout angrily at the screen when a film's resolution displeases them.[41] Some women turn to romance novels to get relief from, rather than celebrate, constricting ideas about femininity.[42] Comic-book readers sometimes root for the bad guy.[43] In short, consumers bring needs to texts that are sometimes at cross purposes with what the texts seem to deliver. And they use those texts to satisfy those needs in unanticipated ways.

So too, we argue, with crimesploitation. It emerged, as we have seen, in a late twentieth-century culture that had become punitive. But it also was a response to a much larger cultural context—Modernity—that traces its origins back to the seventeenth- and eighteenth-century Age of Enlightenment. The forces that ushered in the modern age—science, technology, the rationalization of human affairs, capitalism—dramatically extended humans' capacities to shape and govern their world. But as social critics have long observed, much seems to have been lost as life became more ordered and as new techniques of shaping the behavior of individuals, famously called "discipline" by Michel Foucault, permeated everyday life.[44] Through the continuous surveillance, measurement, and correction of persons, discipline worked to control people's behavior by gradually and subtly instilling in them habits of self-management that made them useful to the achievement of certain objectives like the good health of a population, success in war, or the efficient production of goods and services. By governing the mind in this way, it also deters them from engaging in behavior that threatens the achievement of those objectives. Discipline, though, takes a psychic toll. When it is successfully imposed, discipline narrows the experience of being alive. It enlists individuals as their own police officers, left with an inchoate feeling of having been subjugated.

Crimesploitation offers relief from that feeling of subjugation by exposing viewers to constant scenes of disorder. A production assistant on *American Detective*—an early, short-lived, crimesploitation show—remembered a list that was posted in the room where she and others sifted through the raw footage sent in from camera operators in the field. "Here is what we are looking for," the sign tacked to a bulletin board seemed to suggest:

DEATH

STAB

SHOOT

STRANGULATION

CLUB

SUICIDE[45]

These words all evoke a failure, in some way, of discipline: its goal of organizing life (negated by the show's focus on death and suicide); its use of knowledge to bring order to life (negated by its obsession with the coercive violence of clubs and fists); and its efforts to create useful, docile persons (negated in its focus on humans who stab, shoot, and strangle others).[46]

We argue that in an age of discipline these programs offered audiences different ways to feel free. First, and most obviously, these shows openly encourage viewers to identify with representatives of the state—the cops who tackle suspects, the prison guards who violently control inmates, the vigilante news reporter who busts a would-be pedophile during a sting operation. Crimesploitation programs depict the experience of physically or psychologically dominating the criminal as thrilling. For those who identify with the authority figures on these shows, the act of arresting, degrading, and punishing is an opportunity to experience freedom as the sovereign control of others. That feeling offers relief from the sense of docility and subjugation that discipline can create in everyday life. But because it is generated through the identification with the repressive power of the state, this feeling of freedom strengthens state power. The state becomes the beneficiary, in such moments, of "felt legitimacy" among viewers, the term political theorist Elisabeth R. Anker uses to describe the "affective experience of authorizing state power."[47] When viewers experience felt legitimacy, they emotionally validate the state's neoliberal, punitive response to crime. We explore this process in our discussion of the vigilante dimensions of shows like *America's Most Wanted* in chapter 1.

Crimesploitation also offers viewers access to a more subversive experience of freedom as rebellion against authority. From the surly, backtalking shoplifter on *Cops* to the meth-blasted twenty-something on *Intervention* to the prisoner attacking a guard on *Lockup*, those who are policed and punished on these shows sometimes offer a full-throated resistance to order. In these moments, the criminal seems to have cast off the psychological bonds of discipline, to have escaped the domesticating pressures of modern life. A review of the crimesploitation docuseries *Lockup* captures this dimension of crimesploitation. In a piece titled "Prison Porn," James Parker suggests that the appeal of the show lies in a perverse attraction to the insecurity of prison life. "Thrilling to the couch potato," he writes, are

> the din of hard surfaces, hard voices, hard lights; the big dude hanging heavy forearms over the back of a chair as he tells his tale; the hellishly perfected torsos around the weights bench, where a scowling lifter struts like the creature in William Blake's *The Ghost of a Flea*; the cafeteria slop; the dismal, travestied politics; the top dog on the tier, who in passing plucks a baseball hat from somebody's head and sets it conclusively on his own. Tickled, scarified, the unincarcerated viewer thanks his lucky stars and solemnly wonders after what fashion he might, if it came to it, do his own time.[48]

Viewers like Parker find a sort of thrill in imagining a world less disciplined, more authentic, and ultimately more alive. The freedom in this sort of viewing experience is the experience of becoming untethered from the obligations—and the security—of a disciplined society. In shows like *Intervention*, which we examine in chapter 2, crimesploitation offers fantasies of escape from the very regime it reflects and reinforces.

Finally, and perhaps most provocatively, we argue that crimesploitation offers viewers a kind of freedom from the responsibility of being in charge of their own lives. On the surface, these shows depict the punishment of criminals as humiliating, degrading, and horrifying, presumably deterring those who would be tempted to break the law. The experience of being dominated—beholden to an authority that directs one's every move—is shameful, yet also famously charged with erotic appeal to some. In a neoliberal culture that fetishizes personal responsibility and self-control, the punishment visited upon criminals may offer a different kind of reward: relief from having to regulate one's behavior, relief at submitting oneself to the control of another. If legal and political freedom are only granted to those who constantly discipline themselves, then domination of the self by authority can be experienced as a perverse kind of counter-freedom: freedom *from* the burdens of self-governance. In chapter 2, for instance, we examine the way that the crimesploitation show *To Catch a Predator* flirts with the taboo desire to be exposed and humiliated. And in chapter 3 we argue that some of these shows, such as *Dog the Bounty Hunter* and *Lockup*, romanticize the experience of capture and imprisonment by recasting the pain of punishment as having regenerative qualities.

Contradictory Freedoms of Crimesploitation

Crimesploitation, as we shall see, is awash in contradictions. Summing up the history of classical exploitation films, Eric Schaefer writes,

> The pictures may have railed against the dangers of pursuing plea-
> sure, but they supplied it in the form of titillating spectacle. . . .
> [Their] paean to a stable social and moral order was expressed in a
> form that lacked stability and order. The films reveled in the exotic
> but were exceptionally provincial. They professed a concern about
> education but went about it in a slapdash fashion. They claimed to
> expose truth but did it in a leering and suggestive way. They took a
> moral high ground but engaged in morally questionable practices.[49]

A similar set of contradictions, we will show, characterize crimesploitation. Crimesploitation presents criminals as examples of the dangers of extreme self-indulgence, yet it makes a spectacle of them, stoking and satisfying audiences' desires to watch people engaging in transgressive behavior. Crimesploitation overtly favors conformity to a conservative moral order, yet it appeals to a taboo desire to witness disorder.

But the hypocrisy of crimesploitation is more troubling. That which is "exploited" by the television programs we study in this book is not simply the salacious, the taboo, or the lurid. It is human beings. Crimesploitation takes the most troubled, and often the most vulnerable, among us and turns them into vehicles that audiences can use to satisfy different, often contradictory, desires for freedom. Freedom as control over enemies. Freedom as transgression of boundaries. Freedom as release from responsibility. Freedom as disidentification with the "unfree." Freedom as the opportunity to tour the land of the unfree without enduring the hardships of its inhabitants. In the end, this is what is so exploitative about crimesploitation. Its pleasures are always derived from others' pain.

1

Humilitainment, Inc.

Policing the Criminal on Primetime

When the first crimesploitation programs began lighting up Americans' television screens in the late 1980s, crime policy in the United States had recently undergone a period of dramatic change. Twenty years earlier, liberal optimism about the government's ability to solve social problems through social reforms had dominated American public policy. Many policymakers held that crime was not an inevitable part of modern life, but the result of poverty. Programs that improved the health, economic security, and well-being of the poor, they had asserted, would lower crime rates and make everyone safer. But when violent crime rose dramatically in the 1960s and 1970s, a slew of nationally prominent conservatives—from Barry Goldwater to Richard Nixon to Ronald Reagan—declared liberal, welfare-oriented approaches to public safety to be a failure. Under the banner of "law and order," they began calling for something different: the rejection of excuses and the courage to hold those who committed crime personally responsible for their behavior. Government, they said, needed to get tough. And it did. From mandatory minimum sentences to three strikes laws to zero tolerance policies, the nation had begun sending more Americans to prison for longer periods. By the time *America's Most Wanted*, *Unsolved Mysteries*, and *Cops* premiered in the late 1980s, an entirely different way of thinking about crime control had taken hold.[1]

Fear had driven this transformation in American criminal justice. Everywhere Americans looked in the 1970s and 1980s, they could find reasons to worry about the personal safety of themselves or their loved ones. Armed robberies, muggings, and home invasions filled the daily newspapers and nightly television newscasts where, in an age before widespread Internet use, most people got their news. The faces of missing children adorned milk cartons Americans kept in their fridges, reminders of high-profile cases of boys and girls snatched by strangers while delivering newspapers or shopping with their parents.[2] Fearmongering commercials for home security systems warned Americans that their homes were vulnerable to attack. "I can pick most locks with a credit card" a would-be burglar creepily bragged in one ad.[3] Evidence of the impact of these messages could be found everywhere. It was in the whistles and miniature mace spray cans that women clipped onto their keychains. It was in people's avoidance of parks, alleyways, or even entire neighborhoods—sometimes their own—after dark.[4] And it was in public opinion polls. By the mid-1990s, crime and violence had taken the number 1 spot in Gallup's annual report on what Americans said was the most important problems facing the country. Violence was a greater source of anxiety than unemployment, fear of war, terrorism, or poverty.[5]

In a nation preoccupied with crime, crimesploitation gave Americans the chance to do something other than worry. In this first chapter, we explore some of the best-known series in the crimesploitation genre and argue that they worked to advance the agenda of the neoliberal carceral state by inviting viewers to inhabit the perspective of authorities combatting two types of criminal threats. The first was the evil predator. Shows like *Unsolved Mysteries* (1987–2010), *America's Most Wanted* (1988–2012), and *To Catch a Predator* (2004–7) showcased murderers, kidnappers, and child molesters—cultural bogeymen who preyed upon good, virtuous Americans. These shows gave viewers the opportunity to regain a feeling of control over their world by participating in tracking down, capturing, and vanquishing evildoers. Shows like *Cops* (1989–2020), by contrast, focused on a different kind of criminal threat: delinquents—poor, dysfunctional, drug-addled people who predominantly preyed on one another. Here, viewers were not so much empowered as they were reassured of their social distance from a criminal underclass that could be mocked rather than feared. These shows invited viewers to experience a sense of their own superiority as police physically and psychologically dominated "failed" citizens, keeping them in their literal and figurative places. As American politicians embraced criminal justice policies that would imprison unprecedented numbers of people, these programs made those policies feel like common sense.[6]

Turning Predators into Prey

If the nation's politicians and journalists stoked fear of crime, crimesploitation offered Americans a way to replace their anxiety with different, more pleasurable feelings. Shows like *America's Most Wanted* and *To Catch a Predator* evoked a vigilante tradition in American history that was still widely romanticized in the late twentieth century. Vigilantism—the practice of citizens, alone or in groups, assuming crime-fighting powers normally reserved to the state—had its modern origins in anti-Black and anti-immigrant violence of the late nineteenth and early twentieth centuries. Perhaps the best-known example of vigilante violence during this period is the epidemic of lynchings that took hold in the South in the late nineteenth century. Claiming that the law was ineffective at controlling Black crime, aggrieved white communities in the South turned to mob violence and murdered thousands of African Americans, mostly men, who had been accused of crime. Whites advanced a narrative, initially accepted by newspapers, that lynching was necessary and even heroic.[7] Mobs saw themselves as protectors of communities that the law had abandoned. In their minds, a lynching was a symbolic restoration of a political order that had been ruined by the abolition of slavery and the constitutional amendments that declared Black persons the civic equals of white men.

Over time, actual acts of anti-Black lynching declined in part because new technologies made symbolic lynchings possible. As actual lynchings declined, representations of this kind of violence grew. As historian Grace Elizabeth Hale has explained, from the circulation of lynching photographs to the exhibitions of fictional films like *Birth of a Nation* that depicted lynchings to amusement park games like Coney Island's "dunk the n***r," whites "could now consume a lynching without consuming a black man, alleviating the danger of lynching spilling over into an anarchy that destroyed valuable property."[8] The populist rush that lynchings generated for whites—an empowering feeling of racial solidarity—could be achieved virtually.

Decades later, a roughly analogous set of historical circumstances prompted the emergence of a new era of distrust of government. This time the justification for vigilantism went something like this: Black uprisings in the nation's cities in the latter half of the 1960s had made them into no-go zones filled with dangerous nonwhite others. The government seemed indifferent to (white) crime victims, whose demands for accountability and justice went unheard. The Supreme Court, meanwhile, was giving new rights to criminals, allowing them to manipulate technicalities to evade justice. As an expression of these grievances, a new wave of vigilante sentiment burst into the American consciousness in a spate of wildly popular movies in the 1970s and 1980s. Films like *Dirty Harry* and *Death Wish* glorified white men who responded to the failure of the law to protect innocent (white) people by launching one-man campaigns against social menaces. The men in these films were doing what the state was perceived as not doing: hunting down and permanently eradicating dangerous threats to society.

While it was born out of a similar sense of alienation from the law, white vigilante sentiment in the late twentieth century was different from its early twentieth-century predecessor. First, this new vigilantism was mostly confined to the domain of fantasy and political rhetoric.[9] The grotesque spectacles of vigilante violence—lynchings carried out in front of crowds— did not reemerge in the late twentieth century. Second, late twentieth-century vigilantism was only superficially antigovernment; the populist demand to "take back the streets" was embraced by social and economic conservatives who, far from being anti-government, sought to replace the welfare apparatuses of the state with expanding policing and prison infra-structure. Indeed, from cowboy-hat-wearing district attorneys who made the death penalty central to their political identities to legislators crafting zero-tolerance policies and three-strikes laws, state actors harnessed a popu-list vigilante energy to justify expanding the punitive power of the state.[10]

Finally, the "law and order" rhetoric that sought to harness vigilante distrust of the state was less racially explicit than it had been in the early twentieth century. The villains in 1970s vigilante films were only sometimes Black. Dirty Harry's first big enemy was a white, Charles Manson–like psychopath, a twisted product of the 1960s counterculture.[11] And yet white anxiety about Black crime was never far from the surface of crime talk. "Dog-whistle politics" emerged as a strategy politicians could use to in-flame white voters' resentment of racial minorities without using overtly racial language. Without explicitly mentioning race, politicians could align themselves with white supremacy by tapping into symbols and mythologies that had a racial subtext.[12]

Crimesploitation reflected and reinforced this new kind of virtual, surrogate vigilantism. In programs that invited audience participation in the detection of crime and the doling out of punishment, crimesploitation pressed the nation's racially charged vigilante tradition into the service of the neoliberal carceral state. And yet it did so carefully. Overt discussions of race, gender, and sexuality rarely occurred in these shows. Still, the racial lines of demarcation were unmistakable: the authorities were overwhelmingly white men, and the criminals were disproportionately Black and overwhelmingly poor. In addition, white criminals in these shows often appeared as poor "white trash" or as demonic figures, such as a psychopath or child molester. Their degeneracy rendered them "not quite white," a point of contrast that strengthened a sense of middle- and upper-class whiteness as uncorrupted and uncorruptible.[13]

When it premiered in 1988, *America's Most Wanted* offered viewers the chance to empower themselves by participating, literally and emotionally, in the successful pursuit of evildoing criminals. A commercial television program produced in conjunction with the FBI, *America's Most Wanted* asked audiences for help in capturing men and women who had committed terrible crimes and were on the run. The show was hosted by John Walsh, the father of a six-year-old boy who was abducted from a Sears in Hollywood, Florida, in 1981 and murdered. In the aftermath of his son's murder, Walsh had become a prominent leader in the victims' rights movement, working on campaigns to pass sex offender registration and notification laws and lobbying for a constitutional amendment recognizing the rights of victims to attend and participate in criminal proceedings. With *America's Most Wanted*, Walsh offered a fearful nation the chance to "fight back," as the show's tag line put it.[14]

The show's hour-long episodes consisted of segments about fugitives wanted by the FBI. In each segment, actors typically reenacted the fugitive's crime in a narrative vignette that climaxed with the criminal's escape, the victim's rescue (when the victim survived), or both. Segments concluded with a plea by victims, their surrogates, or Walsh for justice that the viewing audience was told it had the potential to provide. "Please let's answer this little girl's plea for help" Walsh might implore the audience.[15] Appeals to vulnerability mixed with a more pugilistic call for self-empowerment. "Let's face it: the streets of this country just aren't safe anymore, and it's up to us to change that," Walsh told the audience at the beginning of one segment.[16] If the Bureau apprehended these fugitives or they turned themselves in, viewers were rewarded for their call-in efforts with an updated ending to the story, sometimes showing the capture or incarceration of the successfully hunted criminal.

In depicting the viewer-assisted apprehension of fugitives, *America's Most Wanted* cultivated an image of viewers saving the government from its inadequacies. As media scholar Kevin Glynn has written, the show celebrated "the everyday victories of those who rise above victimization to strike back against the combined threat posed by the deficiencies and weaknesses of bureaucratic institutions and the diabolical cleverness of the dangerous individuals who are, as the program often shows us, amazingly adept at exploiting those deficiencies and weaknesses."[17] By participating in the capture of fugitives, viewers could become part of a community of outraged citizens whose common sense and decency was no longer at odds with their government, but instead was being recognized by it. One viewer who found himself living next door to one of the show's fugitives explained how thrilling it was to participate in the man's apprehension. "Living next to the guy that's most wanted was, was exciting!" he exclaimed. "It was just . . . exhilarating, for a little while. I was really pumped up about it!"[18] In the adrenaline rush that comes with "fighting back"—so nakedly expressed in the man's comment—we can see how the show could channel vigilante energy in ways that increased the legitimacy of the state. When the show was successful and audience members identified with the police, they were no longer mere spectators watching for "pleasure or enjoyment." They became witnesses actively authorizing, rather than passively consuming, the state's use of its police powers.[19]

America's Most Wanted glamorized vigilantism while ensuring that it never truly threatened the state. Indeed, the show depicted the FBI as an agency relentlessly refusing to give up and celebrating its viewer-assisted successes. But if the show attached viewers emotionally to the repressive apparatuses of government, it also worked to detach them from an understanding of a government that would use social services—education, antipoverty and jobs programs—to prevent crime. When viewers experienced the thrill of helping to bring a fugitive to justice, they were celebrating not state power in the abstract, but a repressive form of state power that eschewed welfare-oriented responses to crime in favor of surveillance and harsh punishment. Indeed, in a decade in which the state was shrinking its support of education and expanding its funding for prisons, *America's Most Wanted* helped recast the meaning of citizenship in neoliberal terms. Citizenship was not the experience of being both the benefactor and beneficiary of a government that worked to promote human flourishing. It was the experience of being deputized by the government in a war on crime.

America's Most Wanted was a huge hit for the fledgling FOX television network. It ran continuously for twenty-five years, airing over 1,000 episodes. The participatory thrills it offered viewers in capturing fugitives underlay the rise of programs that featured sting operations (*Southern Fried Stings, Undercover Stings, Smile . . . You're Under Arrest!*) or the pursuit of fugitives (*Bounty Girls, Dog the Bounty Hunter*).

But none of these shows stoked vigilante punitiveness as explicitly as *To Catch a Predator*. This show, which ran on the MSNBC cable news network, began as a one-off story that was aired on NBC's tabloid news-magazine *Dateline* in November of 2004. At a moment when the Internet was a relatively new addition to many American households, the segment informed viewers that the Web was awash in sexual predators grooming older children and adolescents for sex. To produce the story, *Dateline* had collaborated with a vigilante organization named Perverted Justice. Founded by Xavier Von Erck, whose character and motives were later called into question by outside journalists, the organization had been relying on a network of volunteers to pose as minors in Internet chat rooms.[20] They then exposed on the organization's website the names of men who had engaged with them in sexually explicit chats. Overlooking red flags about Von Erck's state of mind (he pursued the work so obsessively that he lived a "messy life of deprivation," the *New York Times* reported), NBC partnered with Perverted Justice and set up a sting operation.[21] Posing as underage teenagers, adult decoys from Perverted Justice would engage in illicit online chats with men before inviting them to a sting house that NBC had secured. When the men arrived, *Dateline* reporter Chris Hansen confronted them with the illicit messages they had sent the decoys and castigated them for their lack of self-control and sexual immorality. The segment was so successful that NBC eventually created an entire show out of it, named it *To Catch a Predator*, and began running sting operations in communities across the nation. They also partnered with local police. After humiliating the men, Hansen would deliver them into the waiting hands of the authorities.

To Catch a Predator capitalized on decades of anxiety over pedophiles. Since the 1980s "stranger danger" cases of child abduction and child sexual-abuse allegations made against middle-class persons in positions of trust had periodically rocked the nation.[22] From debunked allegations in the 1980s that Satan-worshiping child molesters were working covertly in some of the nation's daycare centers to the credible revelations in the 2000s of widespread sexual abuse by Catholic priests, the nation's middle classes were primed to see their children as susceptible to molestation. The introduction of the Internet into their households literally brought home the abstract fear that predators could infiltrate suburbia. Simply by sitting in front of their home computers, children had become sitting ducks.

This sort of threat was particularly conducive to advancing the agenda of the neoliberal carceral state. To understand why, we need to pause for a moment to explain the role that the traditional family had played in rhetoric justifying the rollback of welfare programs in the United States. Those who justified slashing taxes and social services often espoused a heteropatriarchal vision of the good. That is, they argued that the traditional, father-led family was, in contrast to the state, the rightful source of moral and economic security. Monogamous, procreative marriages, they held, were more economically stable than other "lifestyles" that had grown more visible in the aftermath of the social revolutions of the 1960s, like households headed by single parents, gay couples, or the heads of blended households. Welfare assistance to those living outside the boundaries of the nuclear family, they argued, only exacerbated the problem of poverty, fostering dependence and entitlement. As a result, conservative policymakers held that the state ought to abandon redistributive schemes for redressing inequality and instead pursue socially conservative policies that rewarded citizens for entering into procreative, heterosexual marriage.[23]

In some ways, conservatives making this case for the traditional family were fighting an uphill demographic and cultural battle. By the 2000s more and more Americans were marrying later or not at all, having fewer children, getting divorced, and coming out as something other than heterosexual. Efforts to vilify queer Americans and single mothers still occurred, but they were getting less and less traction as time went on. In this context, sex panics about children and adolescents became a viable way to advance the family values agenda and the neoliberal agenda it served.[24] While sexual mores were loosening around sexual behavior among consenting adults, sex with children and adolescents remained gravely immoral and the desire for it pathological. The pedophile was a frightening, monstrous, and uncontestable embodiment of a threat that needed containment.[25] Crusades against child sex offenders were opportunities to affirm traditional values and the neoliberal state they served. *To Catch a Predator* did just that. It dramatized the idea that the suburban home—and the heteropatriarchal ideal it embodied—was under attack. And it prompted viewers to fight back—to fortify their own homes and vicariously participate in the vigilante punishments meted out to those who threatened it.

Episodes of the program typically began with a description of fragile innocence. At the beginning of an episode set in Flagler Beach, Florida, images of a child playing a trombone in a Christmas-week parade and police officers happily assisting children flash across the screen as host Chris Hansen tells us about the town. It seems like just another routine day for law enforcement officials, he explains, but "later that evening, most of those same officers are working one of the biggest investigations they've ever tackled": an Internet-based sting operation designed to catch potential sexual "predators."[26] Hansen goes on to explain to viewers, as he does in each episode, that NBC has secured a typical suburban home in the area where the sting operation will occur.

Having stoked anxiety about the susceptibility of middle-class life to moral pollution, Hansen explains how Perverted Justice and NBC have transformed the decoy house into a rigorously surveilled fortress. Upstairs, the viewer sees, volunteers from Perverted Justice have created a sort of mission-control center for the operation. On-screen graphics illustrate the extensive network of surveillance cameras that have been set up inside and outside the house. The decoys, meanwhile, wear hidden earpieces that are used to give them directions so that they can be maneuvered out of danger if need be. While the show is not actually instructing parents to conduct sting operations or use two-way radios to puppeteer their children through interactions with strangers, these practices are extreme versions of what the show has announced as part of its mission: to get parents to police their homes more rigorously.[27]

Finally, with all the preparations complete, the predators begin arriving at the home, and the humiliation ritual begins. Beckoned into the home by a young-looking member of Perverted Justice, the suspect finds himself briefly alone in an empty kitchen. Hansen then enters the room, taking the man by surprise. Initially, Hansen lets suspects believe that he is the adolescent's father or a law enforcement agent and that the two are alone. At this point, many suspects attempt to save face, denying their intentions of having sex with the adolescent. But when their chat transcripts are read aloud to them, many of the men pivot to a different strategy, desperate to fend off trouble. They confess to being deviant, express self-loathing, and promise to reform themselves.

At this stage, the suspect believes that he is being privately confronted rather than publicly humiliated. From the suspect's perspective, Hansen has caught him in a lie, confronting him with evidence of his sexually deviant,

criminal intentions. Indeed, Hansen's willingness to talk to the suspect—
rather than immediately arrest him or punch him or call the police—seems
to offer most suspects hope that they can talk themselves out of trouble.
Some try to initiate a bargain with Hansen. In a confrontation with a
Maryland rabbi he caught seeking sex with a thirteen-year-old boy, Hansen
asks, "What are you doing as a man of God, as a rabbi, in this house, trying
to meet a thirteen-year-old boy?" "I don't wanna do anything that's gonna
further make you angry," the rabbi responds, affirming Hansen's power, yet
also indicating a sense that he can influence his own fate.[28] Others throw
themselves at Hansen's mercy, filled with the false sense that the father or
police officer in front of them might be placated if they demonstrate enough
shame or contrition. They abase themselves, like the man who calls himself
a "sick son of a bitch."[29] All, however, seem to think they still maintain some
control over their public reputation.

They are, of course, wrong. After toying with the suspect, Hansen
announces who he is and then summons production staffers wielding hand-
held cameras into the room. The suspect quickly realizes that he is not
participating in any kind of effort to resolve the situation he has created.
He is instead being forced to expose his failings and inadequacies. He is not
being shamed, for efforts by others to shame a person can be resisted. He
is instead being humiliated, "morally assaulted" by persons who are there
to forcibly degrade him. As Jack Katz explains,

> Humiliation drives you down; in humiliation, you feel suddenly
> made small, so small that everyone seems to look down on you.
> Humiliation often moves through the body by warming the top
> of the head; then moving to the face, where its acknowledgement
> may create the blush of shame; and then working itself through
> the self, ultimately to envelop it from top to bottom.[30]

The humiliation is all the more powerful because the suspect has unknow-
ingly been led to believe that he occupied a bargaining position that was
never his to begin with. As we have seen, with the hope that he might
escape consequences the suspect has been made to dance, so to speak, for
NBC's cameras, engaging in a whole host of debasing behaviors. He is thus
doubly abased: first for his deviant desires and second for the presumption that he was competent enough to avoid the consequences for them.
Indeed, his exposure as a sexual predator to millions of Americans is so
humiliating that it is not too much of an exaggeration to describe it as a

metaphorical execution. Unveiled as a moral degenerate, he has likely lost control over his reputation forever.

When camera operators descend upon the suspect, viewers' relationship to the spectacle changes as well. Until that moment, the audience has occupied a distant perspective, observing Hansen essentially prepare the scene of punishment. Now, with the appearance of the cameras, the audience is reminded that their gaze upon the scene of punishment is the source of the punished person's humiliation; without people watching, there is no humiliation. Indeed, if we understand those cameras as weapons, as legal scholar Amy Adler does, then the audience is reminded that their presence is not a passive one.[31] The camera's lens is their eye; the offender's awareness of their gaze is designed to have degrading and humiliating effects on him. The suspects seem to physically register this moral assault. The rabbi who was, moments earlier, trying to bargain with Hansen stumbles forward, waves of humiliation and shock and defensiveness overtaking his body. *Dateline* personnel move into the room to restrain him after he begins moving erratically. As he tries to stop the exposure, he puts his hands up in a defensive posture, as if to try to resist the reputational death that the cameras represent. The effort fails, the camera's gaze remains unrestrained, and with it, the audience is allowed to do its work, becoming the source of the humiliating pain they were merely witnessing moments earlier (fig. 1).[32]

Like *America's Most Wanted*, *To Catch a Predator* worked to legitimize the repressive apparatus of the state by appealing to vigilante fantasies. In running the sting operations before handing off the predators to law enforcement, NBC and Perverted Justice went even further than *America's Most Wanted* in cultivating audience investment in the act of policing and punishing. Its camera work turned the audience, at times, from passive spectator to active participant in the administration of an extralegal punishment against dangerous sexual deviants. When viewers respond sympathetically to such appeals, they actively participate in the fortification of the neoliberal carceral state. As Stephen Dillon argues, ideal neoliberal citizens are not supposed to be docile consumers; they are encouraged and emotionally rewarded for adopting, alongside state actors, "a regulatory logic that polices those who fail to conform to the racial, gendered, and sexual norms that govern the distribution of life and death" in American society. Dillon writes, "The proper neoliberal subject polices what exceeds the domain of neoliberalism's ordering of life and in this way is one with the police." *To Catch a Predator* was an invitation to viewers to participate in that policing.[33]

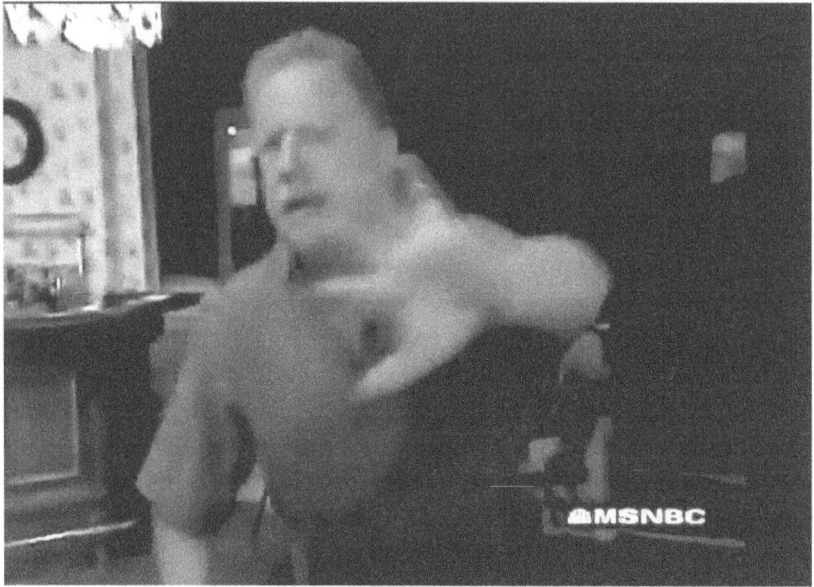

Figure 1. On *To Catch a Predator*, the camera and, by extension, the audience become an instrument of punishment. Source: author screen capture.

Indeed, in each segment, after his public identity is destroyed, the suspect leaves the house and is immediately arrested by local police, sometimes with gratuitous fanfare. In such moments, the show and its viewers become "one with the police," cleansing the show's vigilantism of any sort of resentment of state officials.[34]

And yet the vigilante ethos that shows like *To Catch a Predator* and *America's Most Wanted* celebrated may have given Americans more than they initially bargained for. Its latent distrust of government is not always so easily constrained. In Internet chat rooms and on social-media websites, those on both the left and the right have found platforms on which to portray their cultural and political opponents in demonic terms and to engage in campaigns to humiliate and degrade them. The far right's use of these tactics, however, has had politically destabilizing consequences. In 2016 Donald Trump rose to power by tapping into a populist, far-right desire to see his political opponent, Hillary Clinton, publicly degraded and punished. "Lock her up! Lock her up!" crowds of thousands chanted at his campaign rallies. Trump, in turn, suggested that he might wield the power of the presidency to pursue criminal corruption charges against her. The construction of liberal establishment figures like Clinton and Barack Obama as existential threats to a conservative way of life did not simply introduce the specter of authoritarian tactics into American politics; it also underlay conspiracy theories that the Democratic Party was getting away with rampant pedophilia and massive voter fraud. Spectacular acts of vigilante violence—from the shooting up of a Washington, DC, pizza parlor in December 2016 (to stop a nonexistent pedophile ring) to the January 2021 invasion of the Capitol (to overturn the results of a "fraudulent" presidential election)—were the result. In such moments we can see how the fear, vigilante desire, and urge to degrade and demean that crimesploitation cultivated on behalf of the state can turn against it.

Policing Delinquents

In the first half of this chapter, we showed that shows like *America's Most Wanted* and *To Catch a Predator* offered viewers the opportunity to participate in the apprehension and degradation of folk devils who threatened the security of middle-class people. We argued that these programs worked to legitimize a neoliberal-carceral approach to governance in which the state shrinks social services and partners with "good citizens" to surveil, police, and punish threats to the social and political order.

In the second half of the chapter, we turn our attention to crimesploitation programs that worked to advance the agenda of the neoliberal carceral state in a different way: by helping viewers to make sense of the large number of people trapped in poverty and deprived of opportunity. Our case study is *Cops*, one of the first and most successful crimesploitation programs of the late twentieth century. *Cops* premiered in 1989 with a deceptively simple format: edited, unnarrated footage of law enforcement officers patrolling their jurisdictions and responding to reports of crime. The show went on to become one of the biggest success stories in the history of reality television: 1,100 episodes over the course of thirty-one years. Like *America's Most Wanted* and (later) *To Catch a Predator*, *Cops* could evoke the myth of heroic (white) men policing the thin blue line between civilization and (often nonwhite or sexually nonnormative) predators.[35] Like newspaper and television news reporting, it privileged police perspectives and, when police got violent with suspects, justified their use of force.[36] But if *America's Most Wanted* and *To Catch a Predator* showed police officers protecting the nation from urgent existential threats to innocence, *Cops* showed them engaged in something different: managing the economic losers of American society whose unstable lives frequently put them in contact with the police.[37] American studies scholar Elayne Rapping has described the streets the officers on *Cops* patrol each week as a

> metaphoric border territory—literally 'out where the buses don't run.' This is a landscape of highways, strip malls, trailer parks, and convenience stores. And while it may resemble places we have all seen and visited, it seems . . . somehow more 'foreign' than any U.S. landscape we may have entered.[38]

It was, as *New Yorker* critic James Wolcott put it in his 1993 review of the show, a "warped" version of the United States, one in which people have essentially given up. "The living rooms the cops enter look like crash sites," he wrote. "The back yards look like dump sites."[39]

This "warped copy" of the United States was, in fact, a symptom of the neoliberal economic transformation of American life. As governments privatized the provision of public goods, slashed programs aimed at maintaining and expanding the ranks of the middle classes, and adopted more punitive strategies to combat disorder, these landscapes of poverty and transience became home to those who had become economically superfluous. They were metaphorical prisons, adjuncts to the literal ones that were undergoing a growth boom in the late twentieth century.[40]

Rather than questioning how these wastelands came to exist or inviting viewers to feel implicated in their existence, *Cops* presented them as abhorrent, alien places. To explain why life in them was so chaotic, the show turned not to the recent history of capitalism or theories of structural inequality, but to bad attitudes.[41] Those who ended up in the back of cruisers, it suggested, came from communities where antisocial values and dysfunctional habits were prevalent. When they acted in outlandish, irrational ways—throwing tantrums, losing their temper over small slights, sobbing over petty losses, screaming "PUT MY FACE IN THE PAPERS!" to the cameras—they revealed themselves to be members of an "underclass" governed by emotion rather than reason, slackers in pursuit of immediate gratification rather than long-term security. Culture, not capitalism, appeared responsible for the hollowed-out landscape of transience and insecurity in which the police would find them.[42]

In episode after episode, the officers show audiences just how ungovernable the inhabitants of American wastelands are. At the heart of their bad behavior, the show suggests, is a kind of shamelessness. In some ways, their behavior in front of the cameras resembles that of "rakes," condemned men and women in eighteenth-century Europe who refused to take their own executions seriously. Urging the crowds of people gathered to watch them die to recognize "the cheapness and unpredictability of life," rakes alarmed authorities, who feared that the crowds would take the wrong messages away from the execution.[43] With a similar "nothing left to lose" spirit, many suspects on *Cops* seem to perform for the cameras. In one segment set in Kansas City, for instance, the police chase down a Black man who was joyriding and fled the scene on foot after crashing his Pontiac into an occupied vehicle. After extracting the man from the hold of a dump truck where he had hidden himself, the officers confront him with the marijuana and money they found in his car. He is totally unphased. The $100 bills the officers ask him about? They are "ones," he insists, brazenly denying reality. The officers then ask him how he makes his money. "I like girls is what it is. They pay me," he responds. "You're a gigolo?" they skeptically ask. The man nods, boldly refusing to give the police what they want—a confession to dealing drugs—by defiantly embracing another criminal identity as a prostitute. His arrest is not a moment of surrender to authority, but a defiant performance of self-aggrandizement.[44]

Others treat the officers as if they are minor inconveniences rather than agents of the law. In a segment set in North Las Vegas, police respond to a domestic dispute between a Black man and a Black woman on a street corner. The man balks when the police officer orders him to sit down on the curb and then moves evasively when the officer attempts to grab him. We hear the staccato crackle of taser sounds. Perhaps because of his large size, the man does not immediately fall. Stumbling forward, he pauses, points his finger at the woman with whom he has been fighting, and calmly says, "I'll get you, bitch!" before finally falling down (fig. 2).[45] Nothing, not even excruciating pain, will deter him from getting the last word in his petty domestic dispute.

Unlike those of their predecessors, the performances of these modern rakes are less likely to undermine the legitimacy of those in power. Today, authorities have more control over the spectacle. Whereas early modern executions occurred in front of potentially unruly crowds, modern audiences encounter the performances of suspects on *Cops* in relative isolation; they cannot be influenced by the dynamics of a corruptible crowd. And the behavior of the suspects on *Cops* is more tightly surrounded by material that

Figure 2. The *Cops* suspect as a modern rake. Source: author screen capture.

urges audiences to see the behavior as pathetic rather than brave. The show privileges the perspective of the officers who speak to the cameras about the work they do and the suspects they encounter, working to forestall interpretations of suspects' behavior as politically subversive. As a result, when the pot dealer who recklessly crashed into an occupied car brags that he is a gigolo, his rakishness comes off as pathetic rather than irreverent. When the tasered man resists the pain of electrocution just to have the last word in a domestic squabble, he comes off as comically incapable of reason. While critically minded audiences may interpret this behavior as a form of social and political criticism, the show itself urges us to see these men as overgrown children.

Indeed, many suspects simply appear in a state of emotional disarray—sobbing, flailing around, shouting expletives. The cops appear, in contrast, as "the adults in the urban milieu."[46] In a segment set in Hamilton County, Tennessee, an officer patrolling what he describes as a "high drug area" conducts a pretext stop, pulling over a white man and a white woman in a pickup truck because the driver was not wearing a seatbelt. While he is interrogating the driver of the vehicle, the woman opens the passenger-side door. The officer sternly tells her to shut the door and she talks back as a child might, protesting that it is too hot and that his request is unfair. Seconds later, she jumps out of the truck and begins running away from the scene. The officer gives chase and tackles her. On the ground, the lets out a wail. "How is my fat ass supposed to get up?" she screams, mocking herself. Her surliness soon devolves into a tantrum. Placed in the back of the officer's cruiser, the woman begins banging her head repeatedly into the seatback. The officer threatens to hog tie her. "That won't stop me from banging my head!" she screams, adding, with the impoverished logic of a toddler, "And you can't drive me like that, Sarge, so turn me loose!" Speaking to the woman as if she were a child, the officer resorts to threats: "We'll put more charges on you. You need to calm down; we're giving you an opportunity to." As the woman screams in pain that we are led to believe is fake, the officer admonishes her, "If you quit moving, these cuffs wouldn't be a problem." "Yeah, well I don't give a FUCK!" she replies, letting out the bleeped expletive with a wail. As the segment ends, the officer tells the camera, "all she had was a warrant for a driving charge; instead, she chose more jail time and more fines and costs for her." The rhetoric of "making choices" and "facing consequences" frame the officer as a parent who is enforcing boundaries with a child.[47]

The cop-as-exasperated parent appears in other segments. In Flint, Michigan, a white police officer asks a young Black man why he failed to pull over. After learning that the young man has no record the cop asks a fatherly question: "I'm trying to wrap my head around what would make you make this decision tonight. How come you didn't stop?" The suspect responds, "I don't know how that law shit go. I don't know. I just know I see red and blue lights. If I'd have gotten away, I wouldn't have gone to jail. But I didn't get away." The officer informs him that he "probably would have just gotten a ticket." The implication here is that the man lacks the foresight to know that the consequences of getting pulled over are significantly less severe than the consequences of trying to evade the officer. The officer then notices a car seat in the backseat and learns that the suspect has a small child. "You gotta be there for your kid, right?" the officer implores. "Who else is gonna take care of him if you don't?" After explaining to the man that he will be arrested for fleeing and eluding the police, the officer further infantilizes him by giving him a quiz to see if he has learned his lesson. "What happens when the police pull you over, man? When you see the lights come on?" he asks. "Stop," the man mumbles like a child who has been forced to apologize. "You gonna stop next time?" the police officer persists. This time, he only gets a nod. "Alright man, sounds good," the officer replies.[48]

By depicting those who end up in handcuffs as irrational and child-like, *Cops* continuously impresses upon audiences the idea that crime is an expression of poor temperament and that the police exist to protect the rest of us from the damage that people of poor temperament can do. The show's format—successive segments of cop-suspect interactions—means that we learn nothing about the past or present circumstances of suspects' lives. And the lack of narration means that we learn nothing about the broader history of race, inequality, and criminal justice that so deeply informs these interactions. Take, for instance, the example we just discussed. History explains the significance—unquestioned on the show itself—of a white officer imploring a Black suspect to "be there" for his son. Underlying that moment is the 1960s embrace, by some liberals, of a theory of Black cultural pathology to explain the failures of African Americans to escape poverty. In 1965 the Department of Labor released "The Moynihan Report," as it was colloquially known, a sociological investigation of Black inequality written by Daniel Patrick Moynihan, assistant secretary of labor in the Johnson administration. In the report, Moynihan—a sociologist tasked with designing Johnson's ambitious War on Poverty—made the case that Black economic failure was the result of a "tangle of pathology" that characterized Black culture. Unable to find jobs that paid a breadwinner wage, men often abandoned their children, he argued, creating warped cultural norms and social instability that kept their children—and African Americans as a whole—from moving into the middle classes.[49] While Moynihan believed the principal solution to the problem was greater economic opportunities for working class African Americans, the report's findings were taken up—and successfully popularized—by social conservatives who argued that welfare spending was counterproductive because Black culture was dysfunctional. With discredited biological theories of Black inferiority no longer politically viable, conservatives embraced a more colorblind "culture of poverty" explanation for Black inequality and Black crime. Until Black culture changed, they held, welfare spending was counterproductive.[50]

That history underlies the interaction the Flint police officer has with his suspect. Race was not in the text of the officer's interaction with the suspect or in his asides to the camera, but it was—as superficially colorblind depictions of criminal justice so often are—its subtext. By pointing out the empty car seat in the back of his suspect's vehicle, the Flint police officer does not simply perpetuate a stereotype of Black men's parental irresponsibility; he embodies the way criminal justice, driven by theories of Black pathology, doomed efforts to address Black economic inequality.[51] In the world that officer inhabits, the question is not about the choices made by political elites, past and present, to maintain structures that perpetuate Black inequality. It is not about how the history of policing may shape the Black experience of "seeing the lights come on" when one is driving. It is not about the political decisions to divest from social services and invest in police departments. It is about why an individual suspect makes such irresponsible choices—and why he does so in such a shameless way.

The relentless attention to this shamelessness is what distinguishes *Cops* from shows like *America's Most Wanted* and *To Catch a Predator*. While those shows stoked audiences' fears of criminals as dangerous threats to middle class security, *Cops* often wanted its viewers to experience a sense of smug superiority to suspects and relief that the chaos of their lives was being kept at bay. *Cops* creator John Langley explained that the show aims to present police officers as people who nobly "do a job most of us don't want to do: Cleaning up the mess left by the rest of society."[52]

The effect of all this was often viewer disidentification with both the conditions that produce precarity and the experience of being overpoliced and underserved by the state. Writing about *Cops* in the *New Republic* in 1995, Charles Lane ruminated about how, watching "domestic disturbance after domestic disturbance, shooting call after shooting call," he recognized how "crime and violence are an integral part of life for thousands and thousands of people." And yet he observed that the violence on *Cops* does not feel relevant to those fortunate to live in the better parts of town: "most of the mayhem is committed by people against their own friends and family."[53] A study of college students' responses to *Cops* illustrates Lane's point. Students reported feeling a sense of social and physical distance from the people and places depicted on *Cops*. "It distances you," one student remarked. "Because I think, oh this is there, but I am here, and I live in this neighborhood, so it's not going to happen to me. . . . It makes me not fear crime like I probably should, like anybody should . . . unless I go in those neighborhoods."[54] Relieved of the visceral fear that depictions of criminals inspired in lots of other kinds of media, *Cops* viewers got to be voyeurs, watching with amazement and disgust at failed human beings acting irrationally. Ultimately, the emotional payoff the show offered viewers was not so much a feeling of satisfaction that good was triumphing over evil but a feeling of belonging to a superior "us" whose value is amplified through the degradation and containment of an impoverished "them."

The Consequences of Contempt

In the late twentieth and early twenty-first centuries, crimesploitation offered crime-conscious Americans opportunities to feel a sense of control in a world in which personal security felt elusive. Control took different forms. In scenes depicting the physical takedown of a home invader on *America's Most Wanted* or a (would-be) rapist on *To Catch a Predator*, control came from vicariously apprehending and degrading dangerous predators. In scenes demonstrating the chaotic existence of poor folks who live in crime-ridden, precarious worlds, control came from a sense of social and psychological distance that crime shows like *Cops* cultivated in its viewers. Crime became something that happened elsewhere to people who had made bad choices. Whether enabling a yelp of conquest or a sigh of relief, these shows offered viewers a sense that Americans who worked hard and played by the rules could remain in control of their world.

But crime consciousness, we have argued, was the tip of a larger cultural iceberg. Crimesploitation programs became successful amidst a larger ascendency of conservative political power. For many social conservatives crimesploitation validated the feelings of those who felt as if social changes of the 1960s and 1970s constituted an attack on what conservative culture warrior and 1992 presidential primary candidate Patrick Buchanan called the "soul of America."[55] It was no coincidence that the authority figures on these shows were overwhelmingly white. For viewers worried about the disorganizing effects of social change, crimesploitation offered scenes of white authority figures protecting childhood innocence (*America's Most Wanted*), punishing sexual decadence (*To Catch a Predator*), and keeping Black threats to the social order at bay (*Cops*). As multiculturalists on the left increasingly sought to diversify the nation's self-image and highlight the positive contributions of marginalized people to the nation, crimesploitation frequently offered scenes of white men holding the line against Black and Brown disorder and queer depravity.

In less direct ways, these shows seemed designed to gain popular acquiescence from the white majority to a world in which economic insecurity was on the rise. Those who tuned into the first crimesploitation programs had lived through a turbulent economy in the 1980s. A good number of them had seen their own lives become increasingly precarious because of neoliberal economic policies. Indeed, sensitivity to a world of shrinking social services and economic strain may have underlain the results of a Gallup poll conducted the year *Cops* premiered. The polling company asked Americans whether they thought the nation should attack the crime problem "through better education and job training" or "deterring crime by improving law enforcement with more prisons, police, and judges," the majority—69 percent—opted for the more liberal approach.[56] After nearly eight years of a tough-on-crime conservative in the White House, the majority of respondents took a liberal, rather than neoliberal, approach to the problem—expressing an optimism in government's capacity to engineer the good that conservative elites had been working for years to undermine.

In this context we might think of crimesploitation as an effort to unteach this liberal way of understanding criminality. Shows like *Cops* taught viewers that containing crime did not require more social spending. Most of "us," these shows suggested, have the self-discipline to avoid living unstable, chaotic, crime-ridden lives. And no amount of money would help "them"—those who fought, shoplifted, and dealt drugs. They were the product of hopelessly pathological cultures. Exposing these failed human beings and making a humiliating spectacle out of them reinforced a way of seeing the world that justified policy decisions that shrunk the social safety net. By inviting viewers to look upon an "underclass" with a contemptuous gaze, crimesploitation made it feel socially acceptable for the middle classes to wash their hands of any responsibility for their fate. And it offered those in the struggling working classes—living perilously close to the precarious conditions depicted on their television screens—a kind of solace: "I may not have much, but at least I'm not like that."

But those contemptuous feelings have consequences for those who experience them as well as those on the receiving end of them. As philosopher Martha Nussbaum has taught us, humiliating others is a way to hide from our own humanity. When we humiliate others, we deny the reality that we too are imperfect and vulnerable beings.[57] It was out of a myth of invulnerability that neoliberalism grew in the United States, a myth these shows encouraged viewers to embrace. In crimesploitation land, economic insecurity and the disorder that flows from it are obstacles that anyone with enough character can avoid. It becomes shameful for the viewer to even imagine that she could ever be in the back of a cruiser crying, struggling against handcuffs, screaming "Fuck you!" to a cop. The result is not simply a lack of empathy for "them," but a relentless psychic pressure to hold it together on "us."

2

Watching the Night Creatures

Crimesploitation and Boredom

In a *Cops* segment that aired in 2015, an officer in Chelsea, Massachusetts, responds to a call reporting a fight in the bushes.[1] Upon arriving on the scene, he quickly discovers a conflict between a sex worker and her client. The john, whose fly is down when the officer finds him, is an overweight middle-aged man with a walrus mustache and eyeglasses. The woman sports a leopard-print top. The officer—and the viewer—have entered a sensuous world in which self-control has been suspended and the freedom to pursue pleasure unleashed. Viewers might intuit that the john in this story has thrown off the obligations and restraints of suburban life. The sex worker's night on the job, meanwhile, challenges traditional ideas about female sexuality. *Cops* allows heteronormative viewers to dip, for a moment, into the foreign world of these "night creatures," to escape just for a moment the world of the corporate salaryman or the PTA vice president.

We argued in chapter 1 that crimesploitation invites viewers to partake in the sublime, righteous violence of the police officer or the vigilante. In *Cops* and *To Catch a Predator*, the officer chasing a fleeing shoplifter or the vigilante who lures a would-be sex offender into a suburban home is an agent of order, but he is at the same time an individual freed from the constraints that civilization places on ordinary people. He gets to use violence and deception in order to hold off the seemingly endless wave of those who sociologist Loïc Wacquant called "urban outcasts," and what officers themselves call assholes, "nonhumans," or, in the racist formulation of one of the officers who beat Rodney King in 1991, "gorillas in the mist."[2]

But crimesploitation also offers viewers other, more illicit opportunities to vicariously shed the bonds of civilization. The nonhuman criminals who are supposed to repel us can be remarkably seductive, too. In this chapter we explore moments when crimesploitation's cameras zoom in on those who illegally abandon the constraints of civilization and embrace chaos. For when the cops interrupt the actions of rule-breakers, they drop into a scene in which the players are doing something that psychologists have long told us most everyone in organized societies secretly wants to do: misbehave.

From birth to death Americans are surrounded by socially constructed systems that work to discipline and normalize them. Classical and contemporary social theorists of modernity have long investigated the subtle processes whereby people are made to act in predictable and self-restraining ways—even as they are, according to the law and often themselves, "free." Michel Foucault famously explained how a form of power known as discipline emerged in institutions outside the formal apparatuses of the state, such as monasteries, schools, hospitals, and factories. Discipline works by discerning human capability and then continuously measuring and manipulating individuals so that they become docile and socially useful.[3] Over time, the external apparatus of discipline becomes internalized as individuals begin to surveil and discipline themselves, voluntarily conforming to socially useful norms.

As discipline tries (and sometimes succeeds) at making life ever more rational, ordered, and predictable, theorists have identified a kind of discontent that modern people experience, a discontent that manifests itself in a variety of symptoms—from inchoate anxiety to a sense of existential frustration to flat-out boredom.[4] In what follows, we argue that crimesploitation offers viewers the opportunity to alleviate those symptoms—often by covertly encouraging them to step into the experience of the criminal.

Modernity and Boredom

For several weeks in March and April of 2020, while the world was in the initial grip of the coronavirus pandemic and many in the United States were homebound, the number 1 watched show on the Netflix streaming service was *Tiger King*, a pseudo-documentary crimesploitation series about a war between a gay exotic animal entrepreneur named Joseph Schreibvogel, stage-named "Joe Exotic," and Carole Baskin, the proprietor of an animal sanctuary that aims to expose the unethical treatment of tigers by people like Joe Exotic. The show blended crimesploitation with the muckraking genre. What begins as an exposé of the sideshow world of private tiger exhibitors ends as an account of Joe Exotic's efforts to destroy Baskin—herself suspected of murdering her first husband. The show culminates with his conviction for hiring an undercover FBI agent to murder Baskin.[5] Part of the show's appeal was the sideshow-outside-of-the-sideshow world of Joe Exotic, a John Waters–style menagerie populated by mulleted misfits, gay polygamists, an employee whose arm was eaten by one of the tigers but who returned to the job, and many large cats. For many Americans the crimesploitation of *Tiger King* was the perfect cure for the quarantine blues.

Crimesploitation has long served as an antidote to the experience of ennui, or boredom: "the feeling of mental weariness and dissatisfaction produced by want of occupation or by lack of interest in present surroundings or employments."[6] Professional thinkers have written elaborately about the relationship between boredom and life in the modern world since before the turn of the last century. Philosopher Kevin Aho reviews several themes in this body of thought, from the idea that because leisure and pleasure are so commodified, they have no "real meaning" to the theory that "emotional flatness may emerge from the excessive repression of feeling and desire in a technological culture that privileges rational control, discipline, and order."[7] Most relevant to our purpose is the relationship Aho explores between the fast-paced, busy nature of modern life and the experience of listlessness. Glossing the work of early twentieth-century social theorist Georg Simmel, he writes,

> The rise of the rationalized, scientific worldview and the emergence of the instrumental money economy have stripped us of the enduring values and meanings that gave pre-modern life a sense of cohesion and purpose. The result is a shared experience of emptiness where life is reduced to the meaningless production and consumption of goods and services. And with technological innovations, we can produce and consume more things in smaller units of time, resulting in a life so accelerated that it is difficult to qualitatively distinguish which things actually matter to us. We are so busy, so over-stimulated and stretched thin, that we have become bored, blasé to the frenzy of everyday experiences.[8]

The result is a world in which many toggle unsatisfyingly back and forth between the experience of spiritual dissatisfaction and efforts to manage it through various therapies (such as antidepressants, psychotherapy, or meditation) or enlivening experiences, such as driving fast cars or bungee jumping.

Perhaps the most obvious ways that Americans fight boredom is by partaking in commercialized leisure activities and the purchase of prepackaged experiences, from visiting theme parks to skydiving to "dark tourism."[9] But the consumption of mass culture is the most common form of boredom management. The irony is that mass culture is a driver of the very problem it purports to help people escape; aimed at the widest possible audience, its images and stories work to homogenize culture. As Frankfurt School intellectuals famously put it, "Entertainment fosters the resignation which seeks to forget itself in entertainment."[10] That irony reflects a larger process that is at the heart of modern life: "The consumer and the producer must find new ways to differentiate mundane stimulation from specialized experiences that are unique and exceptional." The search for "extreme" adventures, exotic places, and euphoric experiences—what Aho calls "extreme aesthesia"—produces diminishing returns.[11]

A much riskier and perhaps more effective way to combat boredom lies in the commission of transgressive acts aimed at upending the status quo. The pursuit of adrenaline rushes in risky, deviant, and disruptive acts is a more unequivocal rebellion against the boredom of modern life. Studying the words of those who have collectively engaged in such behavior—the coordinated labor actions of the Wobblies; the social revolutionary art of European Situationists; contemporary "flash mob" organizers—cultural criminologist Jeff Ferrell finds that frustration with boredom is a central theme underlying the desire to disrupt the status quo. Take, for instance, a sampling of quotations Ferrell curates about boredom:

> The Society That Abolishes Every Adventure Makes Its Own Abolition the Only Possible Adventure
>
>   Reclaim the Streets Banner

> We don't intend to prolong the mechanistic civilizations and frigid architecture that ultimately lead to boring leisure . . . A mental

disease has swept the planet: banalization . . . as all reasons for passion disappear.

> Chtcheglov, a pre-Situationist

No more Guernicas, no more Auschwitzes, no more Hiroshimas . . . Hooray! But what about the impossibility of living, what about this stifling mediocrity and this absence of passion . . .? Let nobody say these are minor details or secondary points.

> Vaneigem, a Situationist

We don't want a world where the guarantee of not dying of starvation brings the risk of dying of boredom.

> Situationist graffiti

Boredom is counterrevolutionary.

> Situationist graffiti[12]

The best cure to boredom, radicals have long argued, is the disruption of the status quo.

Crime disrupts the status quo and in recent decades cultural criminologists have argued that a good deal of crime is best understood as a transgressive response to boredom: In both spectacularly violent and everyday forms of crime, we often find a criminal seeking stimulation in a world that he or she finds existentially unsatisfying. Take, for instance, the figure of the psychopath. The term is often used to label criminals who commit motiveless murders. Unable to feel alive and lacking a conscience, the psychopath only feels alive by hurting or killing others. For instance, writing in 1967 about a teenage murderer who killed for fun, criminologist Raoul Vaneigem wrote,

> A world that condemns us to a bloodless death is naturally obliged to propagate the taste for blood . . . the desire to live lays hold spontaneously of the weapons of death; senseless murder and sadism flourish. For passion destroyed is reborn in the passion for destruction.[13]

Criminologist Jack Katz writes in the same vein about those who kill in cold blood. Studying the words of such killers, he shows how they understand conformity to be their greatest spiritual challenge and lethal violence to be the only effective way to triumph over it. For these killers, acquiescence to the niceties of "everyday life" equates to cowardice. In their minds, killing innocents frees them from a life of oppression they blame on conformist inferiors: "after years of playing with the symbolism of evil, they specifically imposed suffering, writing in their victims' blood the history of disrespect and lack of faith by which *others had defiled them.*"[14]

The vast majority of Americans who turn to crime to escape boredom engage in nonviolent forms of crime. Chasing a sense of feeling fully alive, they race motorcycles, tag walls, sell drugs, run scams, start brawls, and shoplift. But adrenaline-chasing is not the only way crime can help alleviate boredom. The consumption of illegal drugs offers a different form of relief from boredom. Sociologists Emilie Gomart and Antoine Hennion invoke Foucault's concept of *dispositif*, or "technique," to draw parallels between amateur musicians and drug users. Both types of actors work to perfect their expertise in their respective "disciplines," mastering increasingly difficult musical scores or perfecting the art of heroin injection, in order to achieve, in the practice of their art, a transcendent experience of passion:

> Passion, emotion, being dazzled, elation, possession, trance, all of these are instances of events in which there is no action—in either a traditional or radical sense of the term. [Musicians and drug users] describe movement in which loss of control is accepted and prepared for. One's hand is given over to an other, and one abandons one's being to what seizes it . . . we do not take "passion" to describe the subject's instrumental mastery of things, nor her mechanical determination by things. Rather, *passion is the abandonment of forces to objects and the suspension of the self.*[15]

Having practiced musical scales or the prepared of the body for drug injection so often that these tasks have become encoded as muscle-memory, the practitioner of drug use, like the musician, becomes so absorbed in the task that time seems to fly by.[16] Relief from boredom ensues. As poet Joseph Brodsky puts it, "A man shooting heroin into his vein does so largely for the same reason you rent a video . . . to dodge the redundancy of time."[17]

Crimesploitation represents a synthesis of two forms of boredom alleviation: the consumption of mass media and the commission of crime. It offers audiences the opportunity to alleviate boredom by consuming the crimes of others, by vicariously stepping into the shoes of the criminal and achieving the relief from boredom that the criminal act enables. Crimesploitation is a particularly potent form of mass media because it captures the desire to consume and appropriate the criminal to satisfy one's own needs.

White desire for the criminal other is partly a racial desire. In the white middle-class imagination the criminal and the racial other have long embodied a kind of "romance of the outsider." "Culture vulture" is a phrase we associate with the white consumption and appropriation of nonwhite forms of culture in the twenty-first century, but critical race and feminist theorists have long noted how white middle-class people have tried to transcend ennui by consuming the racial "other."[18] In late twentieth-century mass culture, the search for the unique and exceptional led many white middle-class Americans to engage with popular culture about racial others who seemed to embody "something vital, some essential quality that had somehow been lost from their own lives." Concomitant with the Anglo-American rise of neoliberalism and the coalescence of crimesploitation as a genre in the 1980s, multiculturalism became a wedge issue both in cultural expressions and political discourses. During this period in the United States, debates emerged over race- and gender-focused curricula in public schools and universities, just as movies, TV, and pop music explored racism and cultural appropriation. At the same time that *America's Most Wanted* and *Cops* appeared, Spike Lee's film *Do the Right Thing* (with its quasi–Black Power soundtrack song "Fight the Power" by Public Enemy) was being assigned as required viewing in American college classes; a rival for *Cops'* Nielsen ratings was *In Living Color*; the Black rock band Living Colour was a critical and popular smash.

All of this made for a rich stew for social analysts taking up antiracist stances, such as bell hooks, who began her influential essay, "Eating the Other: Desire and Resistance" as follows:

> Within current debates about race and difference, mass culture is the contemporary location that both publicly declares and perpetuates the idea that there is pleasure to be found in the acknowledgment and enjoyment of racial difference. The commodification of Otherness has been so successful because it is offered as a new delight, more intense, more satisfying than normal ways of doing and feeling. Within commodity culture, ethnicity becomes spice, seasoning that can liven up the dull dish that is mainstream white culture. Cultural taboos around sexuality and desire are transgressed and made explicit as the media bombards folks with a message

of difference no longer based on the white supremacist assumption that "blondes have more fun." The "real fun" is to be had by bringing to the surface all those "nasty" unconscious fantasies and longings about contact with the Other embedded in the secret (not so secret) deep structure of white supremacy. In many ways it is a contemporary revival of interest in the "primitive," with a distinctly postmodern slant. . . . Certainly from the standpoint of white supremacist capitalist patriarchy, the hope is that desires for the "primitive" or fantasies about the Other can be continually exploited, and that such exploitation will occur in a manner that reinscribes and maintains the status quo.[19]

Crimesploitation was and remains a mode of exploiting racial difference. As we discussed in chapter 1, plenty of the "rakes" featured on programs like *Cops* were Black. But crimesploitation's racist exploitation is deeper and more subtle—more hegemonic—than crass leering at Black individuals acting out on camera. Its explosion must be understood in the context of the race-coded nature of public discourses about criminal justice that coalesced in the 1960s and crescendoed in the 1990s. The "super predators" invented by criminologist John Dilulio in the mid-'90s and invoked by Hillary Clinton when defending her husband's tough-on-crime stance signified Black and Brown teenagers.[20] "Crime" itself had become synonymous with street crimes perpetuated by nonwhite "inner city youth" by the end of the 1980s. Simultaneously, spicy, "rakish" Black culture (e.g., gangsta rap) became popular in white suburbs, where appropriators such as Limp Bizkit (Jacksonville, Florida), Kid Rock (Romeo, Michigan), and 311 (Omaha, Nebraska) took up, as Elvis Presley once did, a profitable form of Blackface.

In a similar sense, constructions of Blackness inform the construction and reception of many of the *white* suspects on crimesploitation shows. Mugging for the cameras, white men and women arrested for domestic disturbances on *Cops* or smoking meth on *Dog the Bounty Hunter* sometimes appear to have already "eaten the other." They act like rakes, performing their own, street-level form of Blackface. Even when they are not performing for the cameras, white suspects on these shows often appear as "white trash": hypersexual, hedonistic, shameless, dirty, governed by emotion rather than reason, unable to control their instincts. Such constructions, as we noted in chapter 1, disassociate them from a modal form of whiteness as pure, self-disciplining, and transcendent.[21] The thrill that crimesploitation's "white trash" suspects offer to viewers seeking to temporarily cast off the bonds of civilization is not racially innocent, for the repudiation of those bonds has long been coded as a repudiation of whiteness. Thus, suspects who appear white in these shows still evoke the "spicier" racial other that bell hooks recognized as especially seductive to the white middle class.

In the pages that follow, we show how focusing only on the authoritarian dimensions of these texts, as we did in chapter 1, misses much of their appeal. Despite the perspective they adopt of the police officer, parent, therapist, or social worker, these shows may be popular because they have a seductive appeal. They enable audiences to safely fantasize, without consequence, about the pleasure—and pain—of engaging in prohibited behavior. Our two case studies are *To Catch a Predator*, which we study from a different lens than the one we used in chapter 1, and a show about addiction: the A&E network's hit show *Intervention*.

The Seductive Appeal of *To Catch a Predator*

In chapter 1 we argued that *To Catch a Predator* invites audiences to identify with the show's vigilantes and law enforcement officers and offers those who accept the invitation the thrilling experience of using violence to reestablish sexual norms that the predator threatens. But in its depiction of sexually explicit Internet chatroom exchanges and its "will-he-or-won't-he?" suspense over whether the men will move from virtual contact to physical contact, *To Catch a Predator* also invited viewers to witness the psychological experience of acting out an illegal sexual fantasy. The show dramatized men's journey to the bait house as a seduction by forces outside themselves that they, in turn, stoked and provoked. The men who show up at the house have been "playing with the line between the sense of themselves as subject and object, between being in and out of control, between directing and being directed by the dynamics of the situation."[22]

At first glance, it seems hard to believe that viewers would imagine themselves in the place of the vilified men who get nabbed in NBC's sting operation. Yet in both its content and its aesthetics, the show created openings for such identifications to occur. The show's decoys posed as twelve- to fifteen-year-old minors, the age of pubescence. The decision to make its pseudo-victims sexually desiring adolescents rather than prepubescent children enhanced the possibility that men in its viewing audience would be able to identify with the men on screen. The offenders, then, were best classified as hebephiles, persons sexually attracted to pubescent adolescents. Hebephilia occupies, for those who acknowledge it as a distinct desire, an uncomfortable space between pedophilia (attraction to prepubescent children under the age of twelve) and ephebophilia (attraction to postpubescent adolescents between fifteen and nineteen years old). While the hebephile's desire for sex with adolescents sometimes became, in moral panics of the late twentieth century, equated with the pedophile's desire for sex with prepubescent children, it might also be associated with the ephebophile's less taboo attraction to postpubescent adolescents. Adult ephebophiles who break the law and engage in sexual relations with mid-adolescents incur widespread condemnation and outrage, yet their desire is, unlike sexual desire for a prepubescent child, acknowledged as widespread (often humorously) and cultivated by popular culture (often controversially).[23] Indeed, ephebophilia has not been listed as a mental disorder in the *Diagnostic and Statistical Manual,* a recognition, perhaps, of the notion that desire for postpubescent adolescents is not pathological.

The fact that these men are seeking young adolescents rather than prepubescent children, then, widened the possibility for viewers, particularly male viewers, to identify with them. Other kinds of deviant sexual fantasies whose actualization would break the law are common in men. The results of one anonymous self-reporting survey of college-aged men showed that 95 percent of them had experienced deviant sexual fantasies about committing illegal acts that included sexual assault (68%), sadism (62%), and exhibitionism (39%).[24] What's more, some psychological research raises the possibility that desensitization to adult pornography—a kind of boredom—seems to underlie some men's turn to illegal sexual behavior. One study, for instance, suggests that a significant percentage of consumers of child porn do not have a "pre-existing" condition of *per se* pedophilia. Rather, a significant number of men who consume child pornography report that their desire is to violate a taboo *per se*, rather than a child-centered taboo.[25] A similar dynamic may be at play for men, like those on *To Catch a Predator*, who seek out contact with underage adolescents. In other words, the forbidden nature of the content or the contact, not an exclusive attraction to minors, attracts some men to this crime. A substantial portion of *To Catch a Predator*'s audience, then, is likely to identify with the particular desires of the show's "predators" or with comparably taboo desires. For them, the show may satisfy a different reason why people report watching reality television:

research suggests that a good number of viewers tune in "to see people face challenging situations" (63%) and "imagine how I would perform in similar situations" (42%).[26]

While it operates from the perspective of the prosecution, *To Catch a Predator* regales viewers with the details of these men's fantasies and dramatizes the question of whether the men will move from the online world of fantasy to the offline world of crime. Viewers watch as the show works to seduce the men and lure them to the house; shown the interactions from the point of view of the vigilantes, viewers are positioned to root for these men to overcome their inhibitions and turn their fantasies into action. For viewers who approach the show as bearers of their own illicit fantasies—legal or illegal—the show offers a kind of dramatization of the psychological stages of moving from illicit fantasy to illicit action.

The online seduction

In each segment on the show, the viewer is reminded that the first interaction between the suspect and the decoy has occurred in online chatrooms and messaging applications. *To Catch a Predator* informs us that adult volunteers from the strangely titled vigilante organization Perverted Justice, "some of whom were victims themselves," "pose as kids online" in chatrooms and wait to be virtually "hit on" by men.[27] In detailing the substance of those conversations, the show invites contemplation of young teenagers as sexual beings. Indeed, before and during its affiliation with *Dateline*, Perverted Justice posted the entire transcript of its sexual conversations with men on its website. In its profile of the organization, the *New York Times* aired the opinion that by publishing these transcripts, the organization was essentially publishing pornography: "They are putting out for unfiltered, unrestricted public consumption the most graphic sexual material that they themselves say is of a perverted nature," the defense attorney for one of the men arrested in a sting operation opined.[28] And, indeed, Chris Hansen introduces the group as youthful "experts" at impersonating kids who are "interested in sex," an inconvenient fact that sits awkwardly with the larger vision of childhood innocence that is in need of protection.[29] Indeed, the show depicts its barely legal decoys engaging on-camera in behavior that, were it not followed by a confrontation and an arrest, could resemble the opening scenes of a pornographic movie. Young Perverted Justice volunteers are sometimes filmed lying down on cushions as they chat sexually online with suspects they hope to invite to the sting house. Unseen by the men they are tricking, but seen by the show's audience, they nonetheless assume the supine posture one might expect a teenager engaged in illicit online talk would take.

In one episode a male decoy gets on a web camera with the suspect and flashes the suspect his chest. As he does this, we see the mock-up teenage bedroom that the organization has created in its quest to appear authentic to suspects: pin-up pictures of teen idols appear behind the decoy. Rather than simply "agreeing" to have sex with the suspect, Perverted Justice actively works to co-create the fantasy *with* the suspect in front of the viewing audience; it puts seductive pressure on him (and potentially audience members). Given the amount of airtime dedicated to depicting Perverted Justice's seductive strategies, the show at times undercuts the assumption that young adolescents are innocents or that the line between enforcing and breaking the law is clear.

The approach to the house

The next phase of each segment entails a major step up in the interaction between the suspect and the decoy: the movement from online fantasy to physical reality. By alternating shots of men parking their cars and approaching the house with shots of surveillance activity—hidden cameras, high-tech, multiple-angle TV monitors, hidden rooms filled with computers monitored by Perverted Justice workers—the show aims to generate in viewers the anxious excitement that comes with making illicit thoughts visible. In addition, the show sets up cameras across the street from the houses, allowing for shots that approximate the point of view of the suspect as well as the members of the sting operation. So while the audience is positioned, as we might expect, to view the suspect's approach to the home from the point of view of the vigilante—as a hunter looking through her gun sights—it is also positioned, at key moments, as if it were the man approaching the house, moving toward the smiling decoy. The dramatic irony of the scene does not simply capture the suspect's state of ignorance about what he's walking into; it symbolically captures what is at stake when one moves from illicit thought to illicit action, when dimensions of the self become observable to others. While the suspect is not anticipating national exposure, he is anticipating the moment of being recognized, by the object of his desire, as a hebephile. "Is this really me?" "Is this what I really want?" hovers over the scene.

In this sense, *To Catch a Predator* sophisticatedly depicts a character (the "predator") experiencing a transcendental moment of "opening the door" or "crossing the threshold," while simultaneously depicting a mirror-image form of excitement in the persons waiting to catch him. In some scenes, the female decoys stand in the doorway of the home and, in artificially childish baby voices, beckon the men to come into the home (one did this while stroking a pet). The suspect's move in this dance is analogous to other kinds of criminally transcendental moves that viewers may have experienced or imagined experiencing—approaching a stranger on a street corner to purchase illegal drugs, entering a hotel room with a prostitute, or exiting a store without having paid for an item. In moderately illicit situations like these, the person entering (or, in the case of shoplifting, exiting) the scene experiences a deep sense of "Here goes!"—a moment akin to the rollercoaster pulling out of the amusement park station at the beginning of a ride. In most cases, the person has wrangled with himself for some time, debating whether the anticipated illicit pleasure is worth the risk. The show thus enables viewers to remember or fanaticize about opening their own forbidden doors and, in stepping through them, concretizing what has heretofore been fantasy.

The private humiliation ritual

The next phase of each segment begins with a game of cat-and-mouse; in most cases, as we have noted, we see the decoy reveal him- or herself briefly at the door to beckon the suspect into the home's kitchen before disappearing into the back of the house. Observing the suspects as they enter the sting house and before they are confronted, viewers see up close the faces and bodies of the men who have taken the huge phenomenological step of "opening the door" into a new world while under the spell of the seduction. This is a key dramatic moment. Up until the appearance of Hansen, that world is anxiously exciting, offering the possibility of an exhilarating sense of possibility. The rollercoaster is climbing its first big hill. But this anticipation is promptly devastated by the unexpected entrance of Hansen, who walks into the kitchen wearing a blazer and carrying some papers (later revealed to be transcripts of the suspect's online exchanges with the decoy), says something derisively innocuous like "Enjoying the cookies?" or "Have any trouble finding the place?" and tells the man to sit down.

In this moment the psychological drama of *To Catch a Predator* pivots: the suspect's world changes from exciting to dreadful, from thrilling to horrifying. The rollercoaster has crested the top of the first hill, but the descent is terrifying rather than exhilarating. Cameras linger on his shocked reaction to allow viewers the opportunity to observe the visible effects of the surprise on these men. Some stand silently for several seconds like deer in headlights. Others sit down and stare at the floor. Others nervously try to affect an air of nonchalance. In some cases, the suspect responds physically, fainting in one instance, or stumbling backwards in another. The show invites, in such moments, viewers to imagine themselves wielding Hansen's righteous vigilante power to decimate the disgusting fantasy of the "predator"; nonetheless, it simultaneously enables viewers to enter the scene from a different position, to imagine the terror and perhaps relief of becoming prey, of being caught. In the interrogation that follows, efforts to move back through the threshold, to return to the realm of private fantasy, are denied. Scenes in which the suspects deny their sexual intentions provide some of the show's most humiliating and squirmingly comedic moments. Hansen confronts the men with evidence that makes them appear ridiculous, as when he asks one man who downplayed the significance of having brought condoms into the house if he intended to do "balloon tricks with them."[30] In such moments, the degenerate self is exposed, revealed to be the "true" self. Hansen rejects the subject's efforts to project an image of himself as normal.

To the suspect, the confrontation with the evidence of his deviance outs him on a private scale. Hansen, he thinks, now knows the truth. But at this point, Hansen has not yet revealed his identity and the cameras remain hidden. Many of the men offer a confession of sorts. These range from quiet admissions, to elaborate physical displays of shame, to emotional exhibitions of self-hatred, such as the one from a high school teacher who asked Hansen to "execute" him and called himself a "sick son of a bitch."[31] Through these displays, the men seem hopeful of avoiding consequences for their journey into criminality. Unaware that they are being filmed and will be exposed to the viewing public as hebephiles, many think they still have a chance of preserving a public reputation. Bargaining with Hansen often ensues—a promise to cease the activity in exchange for a pardon. The possibility exists for repressing the deviant self and safely returning to the self-governing identity of the disciplined person.[32]

The public humiliation ritual

Just as this hope of reversing his descent into an incorrigible deviant seems plausible the suspect's hope is crushed as Hansen reveals his identity as a national news reporter and destroys it. Members of the show's technical crew charge into the room wielding cameras, making themselves visible to the suspect. The suspect's status again changes, the show pivoting once again. Prior to this moment, the interaction between Hansen and the suspect is understood, for the caught man, as private. Perhaps he is just being shamed. Now, however, the scene becomes terrifyingly public—he is made aware that his darkest fantasies and subsequent obsequious simpering have been recorded for wide dissemination. This is not private shaming; it is public humiliation. Any lingering attachments to illicit thrills are utterly obliterated. In a sense, his life is over. Everyone—not just the mysterious Hansen, who might have let him get away—will now know his disgusting secret. He will lose his job. His wife will leave him. His children will be devastated. The depiction of one man's reaction vividly demonstrates this sense of having been attacked; intensely distressed, he covers his face and cries out, "You've got to stop this!"[33] If the appearance of Hansen represents the descent down the first, smaller hill of a rollercoaster ride, the revelation that millions are watching precipitates the ride's steepest, fastest descent.

The takedown

After further questioning, Hansen says, "You're free to leave any time," and the men usually immediately depart. This authorization creates a final turn in the metaphysics of *To Catch a Predator* because it creates the impression for the suspect that, although his disgusting secret has been recorded, the humiliation of interacting with Hansen is now over and he can exit to lick his wounds and perhaps contemplate damage control. But the viewer knows that Hansen is toying with the man: police officers are lying in wait to apprehend the suspect. Scurrying out of the sting house, the suspect is arrested by the police on camera. In some instances, teams of uniformed officers violently throw the men to the ground; in one particularly gruesome episode, they tase a man.[34]

The coda: "Predators" as caught prey

Once the police detain the suspect, the show usually restarts the narrative cycle with a new suspect. Once the show has cycled through a few men, the drama and emotional intensity slows down for a final phase in which audiences witness the entrance of the arrested men into the criminal justice system. "Perp walks" in handcuffs, stern interviews by police officers, and arraignments in orange jumpsuits create narrative closure by reassuring viewers that the deviant has been officially marked. The destruction of the suspect's public self has transformed him into a fragile being occupying a degraded social status; his secret is out and he is now an object to be looked at and negatively appraised by the state, his family and friends, his employers, and perhaps other men in prison. He is no longer in control of his public image.

On the one hand, we might read the psychological thrill ride the show depicts the suspect undergoing as a warning. Once the excitement of engaging in a transgression becomes the terror of being caught, any relief from boredom that deviance affords is lost. Suddenly, the boring life that the suspect was escaping—and that viewers are themselves tempted to escape—seems more appealing than ever, and the ennui of a normal experience vastly preferable to the chaos of punitive exile from it.

But humiliating punishment perhaps has its own taboo attractions. As horrifying as it is, there may also be an unconscious pleasure in the experience of imagining what it would feel like to be humiliated and degraded. Cultural historian and sexuality scholar David Savran has made important connections between the historical invention of the idea that ordinary men had rights and were entitled to certain fundamental freedoms and the rise of a discourse about masochistic sexual desire during the Enlightenment ("the most universalized and ubiquitous of the perversions" to eighteenth-century thinkers, he argues).[35] The awareness that some human beings take pleasure out of being sexually degraded and humiliated was, Savran argues, a by-product of the new understanding of adult men as beings endowed with the capacity for collective and individual self-governance. For adult men, this new status they occupied, that of the "liberal subject," was ridden with contradiction. Participation in an industrial economy required that they be free (and thus able to enter into and exit from wage labor contracts with relative ease), yet the hierarchical structure of the workplace required that they be self-disciplined and obedient to authority, censoring their desires when those desires undermined the demands of productivity. "Aspiring to freedom and reason," Savran argues, the new man of the Enlightenment "must, to prosper, disavow the knowledge that his independence requires submission to an economic system in which he remains a cog, and a despotic superego that has internalized the Law, the Father, and the Word."[36] In this Enlightenment world, the pleasurable, empowering sensation of freedom required painful self-denying acts of self-restraint. Sexual masochism reflected how the experience of freedom confounded pleasure and pain. For Savran, then, masochism was not abhorrent, but formed part of the "very structure of male subjectivity as it was consolidated in western Europe during the early modern period."[37]

Following Savran's understanding of the relationship between the rise of liberal subjects and masochism, we suggest that *To Catch a Predator* is compelling not only because it appeals to a sadistic desire to watch others be punished and humiliated, but also because it dramatizes the experience of being a person in a punitive, neoliberal era, one in which the pressure to be responsible for one's self, to constantly restrain one's self or push one's self to work harder was expanding. *To Catch a Predator*'s spectacular eroticization of punishment appeals to a masochistic desire to be enslaved; prostrate on the ground, handcuffed, feminized, *To Catch a Predator*'s unwilling star surrenders to authority and, in so doing, erotically discharges the burdens of governing himself onto another.[38] If the discomfort of boredom results from the pressure to be normal, then relief from that identity can take the form of not only transgression of the rules but submission to the punishment.

To be sure, none of this is explicit in *To Catch a Predator*. In presenting the humiliation it doles out as retribution to the men it caught and a deterrent to would-be offenders, the show actively denies the existence of the masochistic qualities that, we argue, are embedded in it. Our task here, then, is not to argue what we cannot prove—that viewers identify with offenders and are drawn to the show, consciously or unconsciously, by its appeal to their deviant, illiberal fantasies or the opportunity to imagine the masochistic experience of humiliation if those fantasies were ever exposed. It is instead to show that the content of the program sets up multiple points of identification for viewers in addition to the one it outwardly establishes. And given the degree to which the show invites viewers to identify as the offenders as well as the authorities on the program, we argue that it was more than a flat-footed attempt at reinforcing the neoliberal punitivism that had, by the time the show premiered, reshaped American politics and culture. With its psychosexual subtext, the show reveals something about the desire to evade—through transgression of authority or abject submission to it—the responsibility of constantly saying "no" to one's urges and desires. Through its construction, elaboration, and eroticization of literal boundaries that the men pass as they transform their illicit fantasies into illegal reality, the show enacts a taboo desire to descend into an inferior being who must be governed by the rod rather than the conscience.

The Dopefiend Treadmill: The Highs and Lows of Intoxication on *Intervention*

While *To Catch a Predator* is a psychological rollercoaster ride of taboo risk-taking and humiliating exposure, the show *Intervention* invites viewers to experience the ecstasy and agony of extreme intoxication.[39] The Arts and Entertainment Network (A&E) debuted *Intervention* in 2005. It quickly went on to become one of the most prominent and widely viewed crimesploitation programs.[40] Each of the show's nearly 300 episodes follows a person struggling with addiction through a brief period of her life. Every hour-long episode culminates with an "intervention"—a meeting with professionals and loved ones that uses both emotional and material coercion to persuade her to enter residential addiction treatment. Most episodes cover intoxication by alcohol, opioids (heroin or prescription drugs such as oxycontin), or stimulant drugs (cocaine or methamphetamine). A few episodes depict more esoteric substances, such as "bath salts" or inhalants (e.g., "computer duster"). Several shows portray persons with nonintoxicant addictions, such as gambling, shopping, or sex, although these usually coexist with intoxicant use.

Intervention's primary focus is the fleeting ecstasy and anxious activities that characterize the quotidian life of a hardcore user stuck on a treadmill. Reading against the text's outwardly cautionary tale about substance abuse and addiction is a show that offers viewers the opportunity to vicariously experience the brief thrills of sublime intoxication and the chaos of trying to maintain it, known as "chasing the dragon." *Intervention* richly depicts the whirlwind of an addict's preparation to get high, her few seconds of transcendental bliss, her miserable "comedown," and her desperate quest for more. The speed of the cycle increases, and the viewer watches her stumble on a treadmill going too fast—seeking drugs again, getting caught, worrying about the next dose, getting into more trouble—until she is surprised by the intervention. The plug of the treadmill pulled, a brief coda of apology and redemption follow.

A subtle appeal of the show lies in its depiction of the experience of being out of control. Its protagonists reject docility in favor of disorder. One minute, the person struggling with addiction is speaking directly into the camera or talking calmly to a parent about their problems, and the next minute guzzling vodka behind a dumpster or shooting up in a bathroom, falling over a couch, nodding off on the floor, or screaming incoherently. In portraying its protagonist as sliding between two states—norm-abiding and chaotic—the show depicts a kind of "bounded chaos." Sociologist Elizabeth Bernstein developed the concept of "bounded authenticity" in her work on postindustrial sex work, in which workers provide clients with a sense of temporary relational intimacy that is colloquially referred to as "the girlfriend experience."[41] We argue that shows like *Intervention* offer their own bounded experience. Viewers living an orderly existence are invited to experience an hour of the bounded chaos of heroin addiction before returning to the stability of their own lives, perhaps with newfound gratitude for that stability.

Those who consume drugs excessively are popularly understood in therapeutic terms as sick persons who "self-medicate" to avoid their problems, but they also might be seen as engaging in a tacit form of political resistance. Extreme intoxication produces a radical change in a person: the act of injecting heroin, smoking crack, or chugging a pint of vodka transforms many from depressed to ecstatic, tame to wild, governable to ungovernable. Even if most persons struggling with addiction do not think of this transformation as resistance, they embody, in a sense, an unconscious indictment of the imperative to constantly discipline themselves. Smoking meth or injecting heroin, they confront society in a different way than the activist might, but an equally subversive political potential lies in their behavior. Many viewers likely see speed-fueled acts of destruction or heroin-induced catatonic nods as evidence of moral failure, but some may see it or subconsciously register it as a twisted form of liberation—taking pleasure in watching the show's protagonist put up a fight when confronted by the intervention team.[42] The narrative structure of the show, we argue, makes such responses possible.[43]

The narrative structure of *Intervention*

Like all reality television, *Intervention* engages in "the narrative construction of reality," or the act of communicating human experience using the structural conventions of stories.[44] As law and literature scholars Anthony Amsterdam and Jerome Bruner write, a narrative is

> a fiction or a real account of events; it does not have to specify which. It needs a *cast of human-like characters*, beings capable of *willing their own actions, forming intentions, holding beliefs, having feelings*. It also needs a *plot* with a beginning, a middle, and an end, in which particular characters are involved in particular events. The unfolding of the plot requires (implicitly or explicitly):
>
> (1) an initial *steady state* grounded in the legitimate ordinariness of things
>
> (2) that gets disrupted by a *Trouble* consisting of circumstances attributable to human agency or susceptible to change by human intervention,
>
> (3) in turn evoking *efforts* at redress or transformation, which succeed or fail,
>
> (4) so that the old steady state is *restored* or a new (*transformed*) steady state is created,
>
> (5) and the story concludes by drawing the then-and-there of the tale that has been told into the here-and-now of the telling through some *coda*—say, for example, Aesop's characteristic *moral of the story*.[45]

The "steady state," "trouble," "restoration" and "moral message" of narratives usually revolve around norm violations. In *Intervention*, the focus is on the character and behavior of the person struggling with addiction, whom we will refer to as the "protagonist" or "subject." The steady state of the protagonist's productive, functional life has been interrupted by the anomalous trouble of addiction. After denying or claiming to be able to contain the trouble of addiction, the protagonist is finally confronted by family and friends, who stage an intervention that aims to restore him to the true, substance-free life he was meant to lead.

Narratives involving authority are often "about threats to normatively valued states of affairs."[46] As a result, they can work to maintain viewers' continued acquiescence to the way power is distributed among members of a society, making the status quo seem just and natural. Or they can work to produce an opposite effect: exposing the injustice and contingency of the "way things are" and inviting contemplation of how they might be different.[47] In the case of *Intervention*, the "normatively valued state of affairs" is one in which individuals are autonomous, entrepreneurial, productive, and self-disciplining—citizens of the state and participants in the market. Dependent on substances, contributing nothing to the economy, and spinning out of control, the protagonists on *Intervention* have tacitly refused to inhabit the role that all adults are expected to occupy in contemporary society.

At first glance, it seems obvious that *Intervention* works to portray its principal subjects as pathological, upholding a normative vision of adults as both able and morally obligated to meet the expectations of the state and serve the needs of the market. Their behavior is marked as abhorrent. The source of the problem is the disease of addiction, which lay latent in the individual and flared up as a result of a traumatic event she suffered, such as child abuse. As a result, addiction is never causally connected to external, human-made systems, like capitalism or law, and the limitations they impose on economically, racially, and sexually marginalized members of society. It is never attached to discontent with the stultifying dimensions of a modern world that has been thoroughly rationalized and drained of any sense of divine enchantment. The solution thus lies not in the redress of structural conditions or the provision of public welfare services but in the moral uplift promised by private interventions. *Intervention* functions to make the problem—sickness—seem obvious, and it frames the solution it offers—private, abstinence-based models of professional treatment for addiction—as common sense. Indeed, the professionals who stage these interventions are living illustrations of these dominant constructions of the problem and its proper solution. They identify themselves as persons who are successfully in recovery from the illness of addiction, and all of them have some form of specialized addiction-focused educational training. Moreover, the three primary interventionists featured—Jeff VanVonderen, Candy Finnigan, and Ken Seeley—are now successful entrepreneurs, having written books or established their own treatment centers.

And yet, in its unhurried, indulgent immersion of the viewer in scenes that depict criminal drug use and the chaos that results from it, *Interven-*

tion protests too much. Critics have long noted the show's fetishization of intoxication. In 2006, *Los Angeles Times* television critic Jon Caramanica noted the educational frame of the show was clearly upstaged by its focus on deviance: "Though interspersed with testimonials from family and friends about how the subject's addictive behavior has brought ruin, the footage of the subject, alone, performing the rituals of addiction are the most gruesome and make up the bulk of the show," he wrote.[48] The show registers the pleasures that come from abandoning self-control. Implicit in that pleasure is a gnawing sense that adulthood is a profoundly unstimulating experience. An unasked question lies below the show's lavish depiction of the protagonist's refusal to be a productive member of society and to opt instead for chaos: why is the healthy norm to which she must be restored so unsatisfying in the first place?

Cute baby pictures: The neoliberal steady state

After its viewer discretion warning and previews of the episode, each episode of *Intervention* starts in earnest with the subject of the episode introducing herself and revealing her addiction. The protagonist is mostly coherent during this introduction, although there is often a hint of intoxication such as drooping eyelids or slight slurring of speech. Family members appear on the screen during this first segment, lamenting their loved one's currently depraved situation, and sometimes outing them as bad parents, sex workers, or thieves. Short clips of the protagonist using intoxicants are woven into this introduction, and a text shot is typically displayed that describes harms caused by alcohol, heroin, or methamphetamine, citing the National Institute on Drug Abuse (NIDA). To create a sense of suspense, *Intervention*'s narrator informs viewers that the protagonist "has agreed to be in a documentary about addiction; [she] does not know she will soon face an intervention."

In the world imagined by *Intervention*, there are only two options: persons struggling with addiction must choose between permanent abstinence (through residential treatment and subsequent work on recovery) or death. There is no room for "harm reduction" models aimed at reducing substance use or making it safer. In scenes depicting the protagonist losing control of his body (e.g., falling down or nodding out) and making destructive choices (e.g. driving drunk or stealing to support a drug habit), the message is that, short of a dramatic change, the protagonist will soon be dead or imprisoned.

The introduction then nostalgically gives viewers a glimpse of the steady state that chemical dependency has destroyed. Endearing baby and childhood pictures of the subject appear on the screen as family members describe the cheerful and healthy life she once lived. Protagonists in their pre-addiction lives are always good at something wholesome, such as sports or schoolwork, and are usually characterized as cute (when very young) or pretty/handsome (as teenagers prior to their struggle with addiction). The glimpse we get of this steady state is quick, but nostalgic. Life was once boring for the subject, and its boringness was what made it great. After a few seconds of looking at a gap-toothed smiling child and listening to one or two sentences from his mom or aunt explaining that the child was outgoing and talented at soccer, the viewer learns that trouble descended on the child: some form of trauma, abuse, or neglect, frequently sexual abuse (especially for women).

The attention *Intervention* pays to its subjects' past makes it unique. While most crimesploitation programs like *Cops* and *To Catch a Predator* decontextualize the criminal acts they depict, *Intervention* encourages viewers to connect the subjects' deviant behavior to the trauma they suffered in the past. This backstory invites sympathy for the subject, but such sympathy works to reinforce the show's paternalistic ideology. People suffering from addiction are so warped by past trauma and their current addiction that they are incapable of knowing what is in their best interest and must be manipulated by professionals into ceding control over their lives to a third party. The backstory also locates the source of addiction in idiosyncratic experiences of trauma rather than broader structures of modern life. The status quo—one in which private individuals are understood as both the source and solution to dysfunction—is thus reinforced. The early moments of *Intervention* thus set up the show's conservative acquiescence to a dominant culture in which immoral or traumatized people, rather than structures or systems, are understood as the source of social problems and private institutions (the family, the private rehabilitation facility), rather than public institutions (the state), are the solution to them.

The trouble of the dopefiend treadmill

In the show's lengthy middle segment, the show begins to invite other, potentially subversive responses from its viewers. With the seeming purpose of showing us how far the subject has fallen, the show moves into a mode of silent, voyeuristic observation, which constitutes the large majority of each episode's forty-five minutes. It is here that the subject climbs onto a metaphorical treadmill, as she obsessively consumes intoxicants and acts in increasingly chaotic ways. Take, for example, one episode's depiction of Coley, a white father of two who works part-time as a logger in northern California and is addicted to methamphetamine.[49] Having seen Coley in the steady state he occupied before he began using meth, viewers now see Coley becoming "spun." He appears on screen as a bedraggled adult dropping shards of crystal meth onto a surface in his cluttered and dirty garage and promptly smashing them with a credit card. He then chops the powder into a long line and inhales it into a nostril through a short straw, after which he contorts his face and shudders as the chemicals enter his bloodstream. Coley then directly addresses the camera incoherently before poking at the surface to pick up stray bits of crystal on his fingertip to eat (fig. 3). For viewers who have consumed or observed others consuming crystal meth, the quantity of Coley's usage is recognizable as a large dose. The line is long and thick, indicating that Coley is a serious user. The overall picture is of a depraved adult hiding from his family in a neglected hovel while he selfishly consumes intoxicants.

The long ride through Coley's intoxication takes viewers from his hovel, to hurried goodbyes to his angry wife and worried kids standing awkwardly in the kitchen, to adventures chopping down trees in the forest with a chainsaw. Leaping over fallen trunks and clambering up giant redwoods to lop off a branch, Coley resembles a chainsaw-wielding maniac as he frenetically does his work. Viewers watch as Coley becomes consumed with the desire to locate and remove "burl," valuable chunks of deformed redwood used for fashioning tables or other decorative furniture. Taking breaks to do lines in the cab of his pickup, Coley becomes a tweaker–Don Quixote, hunting through the forest for his prize. He becomes so obsessed with his speed-saturated quest for redwood that he replaces the word "meth" with the word "burl" when he goes to reup his supply of drugs, as in "Gonna go get some more burl."

Obsessive searching is a feature of stimulant intoxication that is well known to analysts of and participants in cocaine and methamphetamine use. Crack smokers commonly scratch around on dirty carpets looking for "lost" bits of crack, and meth users are known to spend hours digging through cabinets or drawers trying to find an "important" document or artifact associated with a speed-induced obsession. At first glance, the depiction of

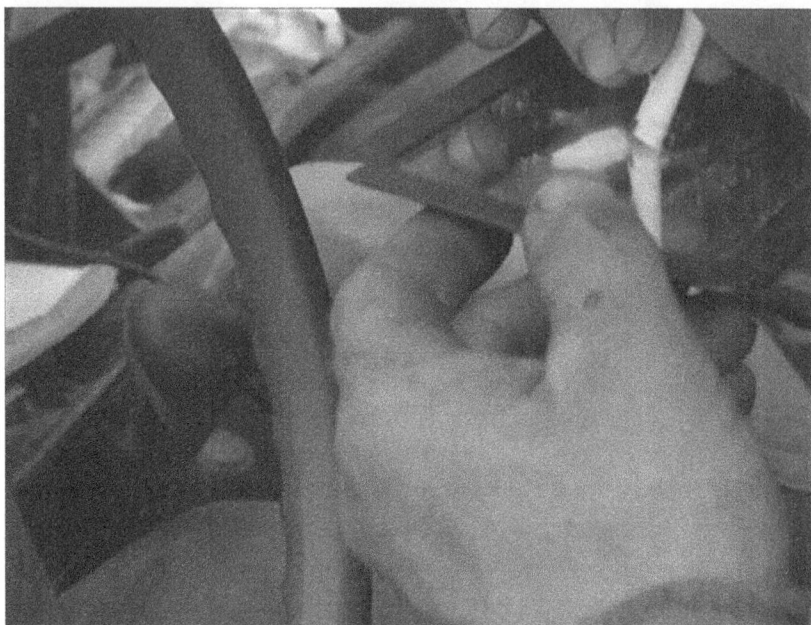

Figure 3. On *Intervention* Coley sniffs a line of crystal meth. Source: author screen capture.

a father becoming, literally, lost in the woods while high on speed seems pathological and depraved. But for some viewers the phenomenon of Coley's fusing of his obsessive use of crystal with his disorganized burl-seeking behavior might be seductively compelling. Coley is doing what the viewer who watches him is passively doing: "dodging the redundancy of time." As he runs around on screen, utterly absorbed in foraging, utterly unselfconscious, Coley is anything but bored. He has become the passive object of larger drives and forces that occupy him, relieving him of the burden of presenting to the world a coherent "self." Writing about the episode in the *New York Times*, one television critic captures the sublime dimensions of Coley's "bizarre obsession" with collecting burl: "His quest for burl takes on epic proportions, and both he and his wife are mindful of the burl-speed connection. There's an unusual poetry in how they discuss it."[50]

Other episodes linger on the shamelessness of those addicted to drugs. One episode features Katie, a heroin- and methamphetamine-addicted sex worker who lives in a cave-like apartment in Phoenix.[51] Because she is no longer able to inject drugs into her veins, Katie self-administers an enema of black tar heroin and water. Viewers briefly observe her preparing the solution in a plastic squirt bottle and then placing her hands behind herself and apparently inserting it into her anus. She then reclines sideways on her bed and explains that if she remains standing, the drug solution will "fall out." In this scene and others like it, the subject's shamelessness is shocking. As we discussed in chapter 1, the refusal of many subjects to feel shame is presented, on shows like *Cops*, as evidence of their barbarism. And yet there is an enviable kind of liberation in being shameless. The shameless have immunized themselves against the judgment of others. They neither acknowledge nor respond to the disciplinary gaze of others. While Katie's shamelessness may outwardly inspire disgust, the producers' decision to linger on it may also be catering to unconscious desire. In a similar way, the show goes into detail about Katie's sex work. As in its depiction of illegal drug use, *Intervention* illuminates Katie's sex work in an ostensibly somber manner, framing it as evidence of her desperation. In the opening montage, viewers see her dressed in lingerie tying up a man lying on her bed for apparent kinky sex to be shown on her webcam. The show may avoid direct shots of sex acts and blur the partial nudity that sometimes appears on the screen, but the camera is unmistakably engaged in the production of the obscene, appealing to a desire to know depravity from afar, to consume that which we should not want to consume.

The camera lingers on the *dispositif*, or ritualized techniques, of Katie's drug use, carefully studying how she exhales the meth she smokes from her mouth (fig. 4). She tells the camera that she smokes "about one-and-a-half grams a day" of methamphetamine and then draws deeply from a large glass bong and exhales huge clouds of crystal-meth vapor. "Meth clouds" are a fetishized aspect of meth culture. Typing "meth clouds" into a Google search returns videos and images of persons smoking real or fake meth through glass pipes or bongs and blowing out billows of white vapor. The cloud is a totem of online communities that celebrate getting "spun," or using methamphetamine to the point where one becomes incoherent and unfocused—mentally moving in several directions at once. *Intervention* provides a respectable veneer to the act of watching a video that, out of context, celebrates the pleasures of becoming incoherent. One critic notices how the show "is almost fetishistic in its attention to the details of [its subjects'] habits."[52] Another writes that "the addicts are shown showing off for the cameras, demonstrating how they steal food and money, inhale all manner of drugs and even, in the case of [one subject], take morphine pills

Figure 4. On Intervention Katie exhales a cloud of methamphetamine vapor. Source: author screen capture.

from her dying father," before asking, "Does this risk glamorizing illegal behavior?"[53] Writing in the *New York Times*, Virginia Heffernan ruminated about the popularity on YouTube of clips from the long, Bacchanalian segment of *Intervention* episodes. These "drunk videos," she suggests, provide "arousal and revelation. . . . Viewers get the excitement of watching people do something immoderate . . . alongside the suspense about how much id they will bare. The presumably sober viewer, alone at her screen, gets either the satisfaction of sitting in judgment or the pleasure of safe, vicarious participation."[54]

Everything old is new again

After devoting most of its airtime to an immersion into the chaos of the subject's Sisyphean slog on the treadmill, the program brings the machine to an abrupt stop when protagonists like Coley and Katie are brought under false pretenses to a hotel. In a drab conference room, anxious loved ones wring their hands and check their phones while they wait with the interventionist. After the initial moment of ambush, the show moves away from the hands-off, laissez faire orientation it adopted toward the subject when it was studying, with fetishistic intent, the chaos of their lives. It moves into a didactic, therapeutic mode. Once the subject is seated on the couch between anxious loved ones, the interventionist tells her that they are worried about her and want her to get help. Loved ones read prepared statements. These letters usually refer to the protagonist's pre-addiction attributes, such as beauty, intelligence, or excellence at sports—all evidence of the potential she has to be a rule-following, productive citizen. They then explain how they have been harmed by the subject's addiction. With the interventionist there to offer moral support, they issue an ultimatum: if she does not get treatment, she will be cut off financially and emotionally and they will have "nothing to do" with her. Interventions are sometimes stop-and-start affairs, with the protagonists occasionally escaping the confines of the hotel room to jump back on the treadmill, sometimes literally running away, on foot, to find a fellow dopefiend or dealer for one more hit.[55]

As seen with the examples we have discussed, leverage is thus a key element of the intervention. Most addicts featured on *Intervention* are near the end of their rope—they are destitute, have lost custody of children, lost jobs, are facing jail. In most cases, a parent or other caretaker is providing some form of support such as housing or money for living expenses such as a car or cellphone, even when the addicted person is in her thirties or older. The loved ones on *Intervention* have power over the addicts and ultimately wield it to coerce them to change from a disruptive force in their world to a benign one. But loved ones are also usually stuck in a dynamic with the addict whereby they value their dominant role and benefit from the addict's addicted state. In therapeutic parlance, they are "co-dependent." Encouraged by the interventionist, beleaguered parents and siblings tell their addicted daughters and sisters that from this day forth, they will not allow them to live in the house or will cut off car or phone payments. Even when the protagonist is partially self-supporting, family members threaten to withhold their personal love and emotional connection from the addict.

A striking example of this can be seen in the case of Joey, a twenty-five-year-old heroin-addicted tattoo artist living in Pittsburgh.[56] When Joey literally runs out of the intervention room, his teenaged half-brother chases after him, crying, onto a subway car. Other family members and the interventionist catch up, surround Joey, and try to cajole him into going to residential treatment. Joey runs away again, and a section of the program is devoted to tracking him down. They find him at the tattoo shop where he works and proceed to tell his boss that he is addicted to heroin. Joey bolts from the store. His family eventually learns that he is hiding in the house of his friend "Pizza," and they and the camera crew park themselves in front of Pizza's house and contact Joey repeatedly on his cellphone. Because Joey is able to minimally support himself with tattooing jobs, his loved ones must resort to a strikingly powerful form of leverage—the threat of going to jail. Joey is on probation, and because he is using heroin a call to his probation officer will lead to his arrest, confinement, and the terrifying prospect of withdrawing from heroin in a jail cell. Being dopesick in the dangerous and uncomfortable space of a jail is a nightmare for a heroin addict. In their ethnography of homelessness and addiction, *Righteous Dopefiend*, anthropologists Philippe Bourgois and Jeffrey Schonberg reveal the lengths to which heroin addicts will go to avoid the prospect of withdrawing in jail—even foregoing a potentially life-saving trip to the hospital because the risk of going through withdrawal while in custody is terrifying.[57] It is common knowledge among heroin addicts that withdrawal, known as being "dopesick," is intolerable without medical supervision. Detoxing in a clinic usually includes treatments with medications such as the drug Suboxone, which relieves the hideous nausea, vomiting, diarrhea, and body aches of withdrawal.

Joey's story becomes meta-crimesploitation when Ken Seeley, one of *Intervention*'s main interventionists, reads a text from Joey: "Fuck you for threatening me just because your show didn't go through."[58] This breaking the fourth wall raises the question, as seen in *To Catch a Predator*, of the cultural impact of crimesploitation programs themselves on the subjects' lives. As depicted in this episode, Joey is aware of *Intervention*'s narrative logic—he knows he is supposed to agree, on camera, to go to the intervention and enter residential treatment. This phenomenon occurs repeatedly across the seasons of *Intervention*, including instances of protagonists explaining that they "already knew this was *Intervention* the whole time!"[59]

A later text from Joey reads, "I didn't do anything wrong," hinting at a legal consciousness about the injustice of status offenses. In Joey's mind, he broke no laws except "being" a heroin addict. After Joey's initial resistance to residential treatment, he eventually caves in to the highly leveraged pressure applied by his loved ones and Seeley, although he convinces them to allow him to obtain and inject heroin before he enters detox. Like many addicts, Joey's process of getting off the dopefiend treadmill is tense and humiliating, illuminating the power dynamics surrounding him, his family, treatment, and the criminal justice system.

Thus, having given its subject one last thrilling yet agonizing adventure in getting loaded, regaling viewers with "just how bad it is," the show returns to a moralistic mode, holding up an all-or-nothing, tough-love approach to the problem as the only possible end to the chaos it has just indulgently splayed out on the viewers' screens. Subjects often put up massive resistance—yelling, crying, bargaining—but in the vast majority of cases the show succeeds in its rescue mission. Indeed, the fight that the protagonist puts up makes the victory even more meaningful. Refusing to settle for anything less than the subject's long-distance relocation to an in-patient rehabilitation center, the show vindicates its simplistic, dichotomous perspective about the lives of people struggling with addiction: There is absolute order (the narrative's steady state) and absolute chaos (the trouble that befalls the steady state), and the subject is polluted with chaos. Nothing short of the radical death and rebirth of the subject in a treatment facility—to be followed by permanent abstinence from substance use—is necessary to return to the steady state.[60] In this narrative there is no ending in which a new, transformed steady state is formed through the resolution of the conflict. The goal is not to change the external conditions that underlie the substance use; it is to remake the subject so that she conforms to the world as it is. The show's conservative orientation—its desire to conserve rather than remake the world—is summed up in its sympathetic endorsement of family members who say, "I just want my daughter"—or son, or brother, or friend—"back."

Tellingly, the experience and aftermath of treatment receive only a few minutes of airtime. The penultimate segment of *Intervention* depicts the protagonist flying to and arriving at a treatment center. Viewers see protagonists, huddled in sweatpants, shuffle into a building adorned with a blandly therapeutic title (e.g., "Bay Recovery Center" or "Clearbrook Manor Detox"), submitting to medical tests and intake questionnaires. While the closing credits roll and theme song "Five Steps" plays in the background, viewers get a quick glimpse of the subjects after some weeks of sobriety, looking healthier as they reunite with their parents, spouses, or children. A last note is shown on the screen informing viewers of the protagonist's latest status, usually indicating continued sobriety or a fresh attempt at staying clean after a short relapse. As critics of the show have noted, the brevity of the conclusion elides the considerable challenges of sobriety, many of them related to broader social structures and conditions of a patient's life that therapy does not change.[61] In the very structure of the show, which devotes almost all of its time to depicting the addict consuming intoxicants and behaving chaotically, *Intervention* reveals that it is not really about treatment or recovery, but the exciting chaos of extreme intoxication and the emotionally intense family drama that comes with it.

Over the years, the show has undergone its own sort of rehabilitation. When it first premiered, some critics were aghast at the show's premise. They questioned the ability of people suffering such severe addiction to meaningfully consent to having their lives taped. They called it exploitative. "An emotional snuff film," one critic called it. "Underneath the charitable veneer," another commented, *Intervention* "is about watching broken addicts destroy themselves. It makes prime-time sport of vulnerable, desperate people and their spiral to the bottom." Treatment professionals spoke out against it. John Schwarzlose, president of the Betty Ford Center, spoke out against shows like *Intervention* turning lethal addictions into "a circus on a television show." Its all-or-nothing confrontations "can add more trauma to already devastated families and addicts, and deter an addict from getting help," one journalist reported.[62] Over time, however, the program insinuated itself into what one critic has called the "addiction industrial complex."[63] Some of the recovery and treatment centers that appeared on the show touted their involvement in press releases advertising their services. Others ran advertisements during commercial breaks.[64] The show's unrelenting gaze on people spinning out of control was lauded for the role it played in generating "awareness" about a social problem that had not received enough attention. An Emmy win for Outstanding Reality Television Series in 2009 offered further legitimacy. But underlying the veneer of gravitas lies an exploitative reality.

The Limits of Transgression

Crimesploitation is as much about the pleasure of transgression as it is about the pleasures of repression. It is as much about the joy of relinquishing control over one's self than it is about the joy of exercising agency. And it is as much about the perverse sense of freedom that comes with becoming an object on which the world acts than it is about the conventional sense of freedom that comes with exercising authority over that world.

Indeed, it is worth remembering that these shows demonstrate these competing desires within authority figures as well as the deviants they attempt to control. While we have focused in this chapter on scenes of men and women violating sexual taboos or devolving into drug-induced mania or depression, shows like *Cops* offer moments of parallel, as the police officer morphs, at a moment's notice, from a rule-bound professional into a warrior chasing an enemy through backyards and slamming them into the ground—losing control in order to assert control. Repression, no less than transgression, can be a form of resistance to boredom. What ultimately separates the energy of repression from the energy of transgression is their different relationship to the status quo. In chapter 1 we argued that depictions of lawful violence work to generate a sense of felt legitimacy about official power. Good violently subjugates evil. Order chaotically conquers chaos. And yet in depicting the lawless evil and chaos that threaten the status quo, crimesploitation runs the risk of undermining the authority it outwardly aims to legitimize. In a modern world that so often feels boring, the pleasure of criminal transgression risks becoming, for some viewers, more attractive than the pleasure of conquering it. These shows' bounded chaos always risks becoming ideologically unbound.

Nevertheless, the pleasures of crimesploitation *do* remain bound in important ways. Unlike in hardcore pornography or "snuff" media, crimesploitation never delivers "the money shot" of raw sex or actual death. Unlike viewers of graphic pornographic films or ISIS execution videos, those who watch crimesploitation are able to end their experience safe from the morally questionable act of participating in misogynistic exploitation of women or the trauma of observing murder. Indeed, as we suggested in the introduction, this sense of teasing or foreplay is key to crimesploitation's attractions. Although it deals in sex, drugs, and danger, it always keeps the viewer safe from observing real taboos and the consequential shame of doing so. As a result, it likely fails to fully alleviate viewers' boredom. Without "the money shot," crimesploitation will always remain furtive and incomplete, drawing viewers onto their own kind of treadmill. Viewers watching individuals such as Coley or Katie "chase the dragon" by frenetically consuming drugs may find themselves chasing their own dragon as they trudge along on the crimesploitation treadmill, impatiently waiting for the next episode.

3

Cuffs of Love

Punishment and Redemption in Crimesploitation

"Physical pain doesn't register with me," Christopher says to the camera. He's a thirty-year-old inmate in Colorado's Limon Correctional Facility, talking about prison violence in an interview for the MSNBC crimesploitation docuseries *Lockup*. "When I get hit, when somebody hits me here, all I do is get infuriated and all I want to do is rip their fucking throat out," he says, the expletive beeped out by the network's censor. He then balls his hands into fists and places them side by side in front of the camera. The words "PURE PAIN," tattooed across his knuckles, fill the screen.[1]

To viewers of shows like *America's Most Wanted* and *To Catch a Predator*, this is a familiar presentation of criminals as dangerous predators whose depravity is as indelible as Christopher's tattoos. But *Lockup* goes on to show viewers another side of the inmate. A few moments later, his eyes are welling up as he describes abuse he suffered at the hands of his father between the ages of seven and eleven, from cigarette burns to middle-of-the night thrashings. Christopher, we later learn, has worked through much of that trauma. He has reconciled with his father, who has "kept his word" that he would never lay hands upon Christopher again. They now have a relationship that Christopher says "has meant more to me than anything." Subsequent scenes show Christopher and his father playing music together in the inmate visiting room and reflecting on their relationship. "We can't change our past," the father says. "But we can make sure it never happens again," Christopher jumps in, finishing the thought. In such moments Christopher is no longer a monster, but a victim of abuse who has come to terms with his past and is looking hopefully toward the future.[2]

In the first decade of the twenty-first century, when the prison population was ticking ever upward and criticism of American punitiveness had
not yet made large inroads into public consciousness, such multifaceted
depictions of incarcerated people were common not only in *Lockup*, but
in several other shows set in or around jails and prisons, two of which we
explore in this chapter: *Lockdown* and *Dog the Bounty Hunter*. These shows
were part of a second wave of crimesploitation programs that debuted in
the 2000s and extended the genre's reach. In these new programs, producers depicted what happened to men and women after their arrests. How
did they respond to capture and punishment? How did they fare in the
jails and prisons to which they were remanded? What did the wardens and
guards who kept them locked up think about them?[3] The answers were often
contradictory. In some scenes, prisoners appear as dangerous predators who
will never change. Yet in other scenes they are human beings filled with
remorse, worthy of sympathy, and capable of redemption.

In this chapter we explore the significance of this contradictory representation of those who end up in prison or jail. In some ways, it reflects long-
standing tensions between optimistic and pessimistic understandings of the
criminal in the dominant American imagination. And yet, as we will argue,
these crimesploitation programs reflect and reinforce the unique neoliberal
culture in which they emerged, one in which faith in the state's capacity to
help people declined while its capacity to punish them harshly rose.

Optimism and Pessimism in the Cultural Life of Punishment

Historically, both optimistic and pessimistic ideas about criminals have
shaped how Americans have imagined and practiced the punishment of
criminals. Sociologist David A. Green argues that American history vacillates
between periods of "penal optimism" and "penal pessimism." In periods of
optimism, he suggests, the culture is marked by a faith in the rehabilitative
potential of those who commit crime. The purpose of punishment is to
help the wayward become moral, productive, and law-abiding members of
society. In periods of pessimism, our more retributive instincts take over.
The purpose of punishment is to condemn evil and inflict pain and suffering on offenders.[4]

This schematic view of punishment is helpful for grasping the big
picture, but it risks overstating the ideological purity of a given age. The

nation's infancy is a good example. The early nineteenth century is remembered as a period of penal optimism, when revolutionary reformers driven by commitments to reason and Christianity condemned the nation's squalid, dungeon-like jails and replaced them with penitentiaries in which the criminal would undergo spiritual and psychological regeneration. One of the most prominent reformers of the era, Benjamin Rush, rhapsodized about what would happen when an inmate completed a stay in the penitentiary. Having counted "the years that shall complete the reformation of one of their citizens," he imagined, members of a community would rejoice at his release from prison. "I behold them running to meet him on the day of his deliverance. His friends and family bathe his cheeks with tears of joy; and the universal shout of the neighborhood is, 'This our brother was lost, and is found—was dead and is alive.'"[5]

And yet to describe the era as one of penal optimism is to miss how such optimism was built on a logic of exclusion and harsh treatment. Administrators of Eastern State Penitentiary in Philadelphia, perhaps the most famous exemplar of the age's penal optimism, argued that Black men had constitutions that made them unamenable to rehabilitation. And those white men who were the beneficiaries of the reformers' "benevolence" found that optimism about their capacity for rehabilitation did not protect them from pain and suffering. Isolation in single, windowless, soundproof cells, experienced by inmates as torturous, was at the heart of the rehabilitative philosophy underlying Eastern State.[6] Literary scholar Caleb Smith reveals the mix of uplift and degradation that was characteristic of the era. In the "poetics of the penitentiary" that emerged during the period, the prisoner's old self was treated roughly so that a redeemed one could emerge in its stead. In the minds of its creators, the penitentiary would be

> a "living tomb" of servitude and degradation as well as the space of the citizen-subject's dramatic reanimation. Its legal codes divested the convict of rights; its ritualized disciplinary practices stripped away his identity; it exposed him to arbitrary and discretionary violence at the hands of his keepers; it buried him alive in a solitary cell. But it also promised him a glorious return to citizenship and humanity. It mortified the body, but it also claimed to renovate the soul.[7]

Violence and degradation thus lay at the heart of an optimistic vision of what the prison could do, complicating any clear distinction, at least from the perspective of the prisoner, between moments of optimism and pessimism.

In ways that have gone unrecognized, a similar mix of optimism and pessimism has characterized the cultural life of punishment in the era of mass incarceration. To be sure, pessimism has dominated many discussions about punishment in the last fifty years. Criminologists became increasingly skeptical of the state's ability to rehabilitate criminals.[8] Politicians bolstered their reputations by demonizing criminals as animals and psychopaths. Harsh punishment flourished in a political climate of cynicism and retributivism. But in the late twentieth century, we also witnessed the dramatic expansion of evangelical Christian prison ministries aimed at converting and redeeming the souls of incarcerated men and women. These private operations were built on optimism about criminals' capacity for redemption. Evangelicals were skeptical of the ability of a Godless, secular government to rehabilitate prisoners. But they were confident that they could rehabilitate inmates by helping them become born again in Christ.[9] Their optimism about the rehabilitative potential of prisoners, moreover, was not isolated and exceptional. It had a counterpart in popular culture. As we will see in the sections to come, crimesploitation popularized evangelical optimism that private, personal interventions, rather than structural change, could positively transform the lives of prisoners.

At first glance, the optimistic visions of inmates as redeemable may appear to counter the spirit of harsh punishment. But we argue that they have perversely worked to justify harsh treatment. Humanizing portrayals of inmates on programs like *Lockup*, *Lockdown*, and *Dog the Bounty Hunter* do little to undermine the logic and practice of harsh punishment. Instead, by showing the prison as a place where many inmates "suffer into truth," as the ancient Greek tragedist Aeschylus would put it, these prison crimesploitation shows suggest that the pains of imprisonment are growth inspiring. In the pages to come, we argue that such messages work to make harsh punishment more justifiable, more meaningful, and even more satisfying to the public.

Pure Pain: *Lockup* and *Lockdown*

Lockup was perhaps the best known of a new spate of crimesploitation programming that arrived in the 2000s to give audiences a close-up look at life behind bars. After launching in 2005 on the cable news network MSNBC, the show quickly became a hit. By 2011, one critic noted, *Lockup* had become a kind of golden handcuffs for the cable news network, which was trying to compete with CNN and Fox News. "The show has become such a phenomenon that its schedulers can't help running it hour upon hour upon hour," Jack Curry wrote in the *Washington Post*. The lowbrow show had become akin to a "crazy rich uncle . . . the relative whose gifts you accept, but whom you keep stowed away in the attic."[10] Its success likely caught the eyes of producers at competing channels. *Lockdown*, launched in 2006 by the National Geographic Channel, followed a nearly identical format.

Like crimesploitation that focused on policing and catching criminals, *Lockup* and *Lockdown* frequently adopted a pessimistic view of inmates, one that holds that "certain criminals are 'simply wicked' . . . and have no calls on our fellow feeling."[11] Producers of these shows dedicated a significant portion of each episode to constructing prison in Hobbesian terms. Viewers learn that, thanks to the predatory nature of the captives and the tenuous control that the state has over the inmates, life behind bars is nasty, brutal, and—if one does not learn its invisible rules—short. Nobody behind the walls cares about human dignity; instead, reputation, hard won and easily lost, determines how one fares. "In here, you can't really appear weak in front of everybody," an inmate explains; predators are everywhere.[12] Prisoners brag to the cameras about how they dominate the weak. "If I'm having a bad day, I just walk into a cell and say, 'Listen, bro, you're going to give me your whole entire commissary or I'm going to beat the shit out of you and shove your head in the toilet and flush it. I've done it to a lot of people," an inmate explains in one interview.[13] The logo for *Lockup*, a fortress surrounded by layers of cinderblock walls and barbed-wire fences, visually conveys the danger that lies within.

In interviews guards reinforce the idea that prison is an uncivilized space. Many episodes feature displays of the homemade knives, bats, and other kinds of weapons that authorities regularly confiscate from inmates. In such a setting, the narrator explains, "inmates must always be prepared for battle." Guards too. "We're dealing with rapists and murderers. That's always in the back of my mind," one guard says. "If you show inmates fear, they feed on it," another warns.[14] "I know what the potential of these guys are," a guard at Ironwood State Prison tells the cameras in one episode. "They work out all day long. They're built. They're strong. And they'll fight. They'll fight to the end." Indeed, the show pays particular attention to inmates who brag about being sadistic, predatorial, and unpredictable. Take, for instance, Jeremy, an inmate in Orange County (California) Jail awaiting trial for multiple home invasions and an assault on a police officer. "I don't believe in drive-bys," Jeremy says in an interview. "I believe in knocking on people's doors and walking in people's houses. To actually get up in someone's face and do something to them. That's when you become numb. Once you do it, you can do it for the rest of your life."[15] Another inmate calls himself a "fight master. I'm like a Picasso with these things," he says, pointing to his fists. "I will dress your ass up real good. And if you give me a blade or a burner, I make a masterpiece."[16] Critics of *Lockup* have condemned its focus on violence, arguing that it reinforces viewers' stereotypes of criminals as incorrigible. In many scenes, it seems, viewers are left with the impression that all they can reasonably expect the government to do is to contain dangerous people—to metaphorically, and sometimes literally, keep them on leashes (fig. 5).[17]

But for some viewers, crimesploitation that only presents life in the prison as a never-ending cycle of violence is unsatisfying. In 2008 *New York Daily News* commentator David Hinckley wrote about a special edition of *Lockup* he had recently watched, one that was dedicated exclusively to serving up "graphic vignettes of violence at prisons the series has visited, from Alabama to Alaska." Scene after scene of violence made for an unsatisfying viewing experience. For an hour, Hinckley noted, the show depicted nothing but "individuals who seem so psychotic, they seemingly would respond to nothing" but brute force. As a result, "the whole episode somehow doesn't seem as interesting, or as informative, as the ones that take a more measured look at life behind bars. It functions more as a carnival barker, flashing the 'good stuff' to get the viewer to come inside the tent." In undiluted form, Hinckley suggested, the violence was dehumanizing and demoralizing to watch.[18]

The producers of *Lockup* seemed to grasp this point. Violence-centered "special edition" episodes were rare, and they seemed aimed at a small subset of viewers hungry for mayhem. Casting a wider net, the show's regular episodes balanced scenes of violence with scenes of prisoners trying to turn their lives around or engage in creative ways to make life in prison more bearable. Scenes in prisons' visiting rooms often reminded viewers that many of the inmates who appear on the show are not just convicts, but someone's son or brother or father. One episode of *Lockup* begins with a scene of a young man meeting with his father in the visiting room at Limon Correctional Facility in Colorado. The young inmate is serving a forty-eight-year sentence for a terrible crime: shaking a seven-month-old baby to death. But

Figure 5. In segments set in maximum-security units, *Lockup* uses visuals like this one, an inmate being led to recreation on a leash, to illustrate how dangerous some inmates are. Source: author screen capture.

rather than dwell on the horrifying nature of the crime, *Lockup* asks viewers to think about what they would do if their own son killed a baby. The inmate's father explains that he used to have a view of violent criminals as irredeemable. "When it's other people [committing heinous crimes], I want you to go ahead and put them under the prison," he says. "But it's my son. So how am I supposed to look at that? He's my son, so I'm not supposed to feel the same way. I don't know. It's been a long road. And I can't turn my back on him. He's mine."[19] Briefly seeing the criminal through the eyes of his father, viewers are invited to consider the idea that a prisoner is worthy of love no matter what he has done.

Indeed, while the show traffics in menacing appearances, it also frequently reminds viewers that looks can be deceiving. Take, for instance, inmates' bodies. Critics of *Lockup* have argued that "focusing on offenders with physical stigmata, such as excessive tattooing, is a way to reinforce the image of 'the other.'"[20] But the program spends a good deal of time reinforcing older rehabilitative ideals of prisoners as complex individuals whose present condition or appearance cannot totally define them. In one episode an inmate whose face is covered with tattoos tells his interviewer that he knows that the ink signifies criminality, but he insists that it is only skin-deep. Gesturing toward his tattoo-covered face, he tells us that his girlfriend "doesn't buy it when she sees all this." The show humanizes other inmates by giving viewers a glimpse of the lives they lived before prison. One inmate, initially presented as a gang murderer, shows photographs of his mother and tears up as he talks about his past. In prison, he says, "you don't have no loved ones you can embrace."[21] Other inmates hold up pictures to the camera of themselves outside of the prison—like the inmate who shows himself at a bodybuilding competition—reminding viewers that they are encountering prisoners in a carceral context that does not totally define who they are.[22] Indeed, in numerous scenes in *Lockup* and *Lockdown*, the prison serves as a foil against which inmates sympathetically assert their humanity. "I'm an addict, but that's not all I am," a young woman jailed for a probation violation insists during an interview for *Lockdown*. "Not being defined as an individual is the hardest part of being here."[23]

Going beyond these humanizing gestures, these programs sometimes embrace the ideal of rehabilitation. We see volunteers working with inmates to help redeem themselves. In one episode, we are introduced to an English professor who runs a program called "Shakespeare in the SHU [Secure Housing Unit]." She sits in a folding chair in the middle of a hallway lined by solitary confinement cells. Through slots, the occupants of the cells read *Macbeth* aloud with her, pausing periodically to discuss it. Reflecting on his decision to participate in the class, one of her students explains to the camera, through his food slot, "This place is built for you to come out in one of two ways: hard as the cement that you are encaged in or soft as the grass you walk on when you leave here." By participating in the Shakespeare course, he says, he avoids both the softness of institutionalization and the hardness of Darwinian survivalism. Discussing Shakespeare, he says, "keeps men from suffocating."[24] A different episode features Jim, an inmate-turned-teacher who proudly tells the camera that he has partnered with a local community college to create an education program for the inmates. Four hundred inmates have attended college classes, he notes, before rattling off hopeful statistics. "It costs $42,800 a year to lock up prisoners. We can educate them for around $800." Seventy-two percent of prisoners who don't take classes, he asserts, return to prison. "I have a return rate of 22 percent. At least try my way."[25]

In *Lockup* and *Lockdown*, then, the prison is not only a carceral state of nature, but also a site of regeneration and rebirth. Take, for instance, an episode of *Lockdown* titled "Inside the Kill Fence." Throughout the course of the episode, viewers are told about the high-voltage fence that surrounds the prison. A narrator informs the viewer that the fence keeps the prison a "fortress, built to be escape proof." Inmates know that if they touch the fence, it will give them a shock that will knock them down. If they try a second time, the narrator ominously intones, the fence is programmed to give them a lethal jolt. Journeying inside the "kill fence," however, viewers become privy to a kind of spiritual rebirth. There, they meet John, whose life has been changed by a program that pairs inmates with abused dogs for the purpose of rehabilitating the dogs. The warden admits to the cameras that his initial reaction to the program was "it'll never work. The animals will be misused. It can't happen. These individuals are violent." But he was wrong, the warden says. The program has transformed John, a meth dealer who has been in and out of trouble his whole life and has anger management issues. "To be in the dog program, I'm re-teaching myself how to deal with people and daily life in general."[26]

These sorts of segments on educational, religious, and therapeutic programs, staffed by caring emissaries from the world beyond the barbed wire, demonstrate the existence of spaces within the prison that negate the image of it as a warehouse. One leader of a substance-abuse support group, herself a former inmate, explains after a scene depicting group therapy for female prisoners that "some of these ladies haven't cried in many years, and when we see the tears, we know it's cleansing them and helping them become productive members of society. And it's very important that we hug them; that way they know they're doing the right thing."[27] The therapy is not always formal, *Lockup* suggests. It can come from the rapport inmates have with guards. Countering the voices of guards who speak of the inmates as "rapists and murderers," one guard proudly tells the camera that he brought an inmate he supervises a copy of the book *Man's Search for Meaning*.[28]

One might think that the presence of inmates who are experiencing growth and demonstrating introspection undermines penal pessimism. And yet, in an era in which penal pessimism had become "common sense," the optimistic stories that appear on these shows fail to subvert the status quo because they focus on the unique particulars of individual experiences at the expense of a wider consideration of social patterns of injustice and inequality.[29] Whether they are presented as mad dogs or penitent souls, the source underlying the confinement of inmates on *Lockup* and *Lockdown* is never identified. It is never connected to sentencing reform or drug policy or the neoliberal reordering of economic life. It is always, at best, the result of bad choices. As a result, the show depicts inmates who are on a path to redemption not as beneficiaries of remedial, state-facilitated investment in their well-being but as exceptions who have been moved by chance encounters with guards, epiphanies in group therapy, or the shock of incarceration. The source of both their crime and their rehabilitation is personal rather than structural.[30]

When structures are referenced in these shows, they appear as "the way things inevitably are" instead of the result of decisions Americans have made about how to manage social problems. In numerous episodes, we learn that jails are overcrowded with people suffering from addiction and mental illness. In an episode of *Lockdown* set in the Portland, Oregon, city jail, viewers meet a man named Lyman who was caught shoplifting to support a heroin addiction. He is undergoing withdrawal in an isolation cell, assisted by medical staff. The narrator informs viewers, "Medical professionals explain they don't have the resources to provide the withdrawal medicines indefinitely" to Lyman, who will inevitably be released only to cycle back into the jail. Another man, mentally ill and physically out of control, is brought into the jail and placed in an isolation cell. "State budget cuts forced many of Portland's mental health facilities to close," we learn. Finally, a woman charged with cocaine possession is admitted to the jail after having relapsed while she was participating in a court-ordered rehabilitation program. When she begs the judge for one more chance, the prosecutor objects, citing the long waiting list of others for the rehab program. Her deferred sentence, ten days in jail and a felony on her record, is reinstated.[31]

Each of these individual stories might be connected to a broader neoliberal divestment from welfare-oriented approaches to solving social problems and investment in criminal justice infrastructure. None are. Left unstated is the state's failure to treat addiction as a disease rather than a crime, its refusal to provide universal healthcare to citizens, its failure to recognize the destabilizing effects of an economy in which the poor have little hope of moving into the middle classes. Indeed, writing about how *Lockup* portrayed life in the Fairfax, Virginia, County Jail, a reporter for the *Washington Post* complained that the show gawked at, rather than contextualized, an inmate's psychological breakdown. "There was no deeper plunge into the issue of mental illness. . . . It is undisputed that our jails and prisons are the largest centers for the mentally ill, by default."[32] But questions about the history or significance of that fact are absent in *Lockup* and *Lockdown*.

Dog the Bounty Hunter

Shows like *Lockup* and *Lockdown*, as we have seen, were designed for audiences who wanted to see optimistic as well as pessimistic representations of prisoners. But no crimesploitation program satisfied a hunger to see inmates as redeemable more than the A&E network's most watched show, *Dog the Bounty Hunter*. Over the course of 246 episodes that aired from 2004 to 2012, the show chronicled Duane "The Dog" Chapman running his family business, Da Kine Bail Bonds, on the Hawaiian island of Oahu with his girlfriend Beth (who became his wife in 2006), some of his adult children (he has twelve children from four marriages), and his fictive kin (most notably, a man named Tim "Youngblood" Chapman who is identified as Dog's brother but is of no blood relation to Chapman).[33] Drawing up to three million viewers per episode, the family chased down men and women who had violated the conditions of their bail. After they caught their prey and before they handed them over to officials at the local jail, however, they engaged in quick, backseat-of-the-SUV counseling sessions aimed at transforming their fugitives' lives.[34] *Dog* popularized an evangelical Christian response to those who commit crime, one that sought to balance justice with compassion.[35] Brushing the tears out of his eyes during a 2005 interview with talk show host Montel Williams, Chapman explained that he was on a mission from God:

> I asked the Lord one time, "Who am I in charge of?" And I went to sleep. In the dream, I dreamed about Christ being crucified with two people next to him, and above it, it said "thieves." And as I woke up, God said, "Those are the people you're in charge of—the thieves, the murderers, the rapists, the criminals. Those are your people." And I thought, "Boy, that's kind of bad, ain't it?" And then I read the scripture that said, "The first shall be last and the last shall be first." I said, "Well, my guys are going to get in line first." And I realized that was my calling.[36]

At the same time, Chapman regularly espoused a politics of personal responsibility that underlie conservative, retributive responses to criminal wrongdoing. The result was a show in which a religious imperative to punish the wicked is tempered by a desire to save their souls.[37]

Most half-hour episodes of the show follow the same basic plot. At the beginning of every episode, the Chapmans discuss the fugitive they are planning to capture as dangerous and imagine his or her capture with a bit of sadistic delight. They describe the fugitive as polluted ("dirt," "scumbag"), subhuman ("bitch," "tiger"), or pathological ("liar," "dangerous"). In one episode, the fugitive has a heroin addiction. To raise the stakes of apprehending the man, the family speculates about his HIV status. "What if he's got AIDS?" Beth asks as they make a plan to capture him. "What if he sticks you with his needle?" Dog reassures her, "He ain't gonna be able to stick nobody; he's going to go down in a hail of mace."[38] The fugitive is a pollutant, "matter out of place," as anthropologist Mary Douglas would put it, and the bounty hunter a heroic handler of toxic waste.[39]

Sadism and disgust frequently creep into these early scenes. In one episode, for instance, Dog asks, during a briefing on that week's fugitive, "Whose life are we going to ruin today?" Beth, meanwhile, mocks the excuses liberals give for bad behavior. She mimics one fugitive's mother, "My son who escaped—he's just so misunderstood!" The family celebrates the act of bounty hunting as a way to legally hunt others for sport. One of Dog's associates hopes that the fugitive will try to flee arrest: "If this guy don't run can we tell him to run? 'Cuz I gotta work out some kinks, man." The hunt then begins when the family piles into their SUVs and heads out to find their fugitive. As they act on tips and move from one location to the next, members of the family take turns making adrenaline-stimulating statements to the cameras and one another, producing anticipation of an exciting, risky, and dangerous physical confrontation. As one family member puts it, "I just get very anxious as I'm waiting. It's kind of like being on a rollercoaster as you're going up that hill—click, click, click, click. Your butterflies get coming. You know you're coming to the [top of the] hill. You're getting ready to fly over the side."[40] The moment of takedown and its immediate aftermath represents the climax—a period of exhilaration earlier scenes have anticipated. At times, the take-down is a small-scale degradation ceremony. "In Donald Trump's words, 'You're fired!'" Dog gleefully says to one fugitive he has just apprehended. The hunters often narrate their state of mind: "We're still coming down," one says to the camera after an apprehension. "We just jumped out of a plane with a parachute and we haven't pulled the cord yet."[41]

Once the excitement of the capture dissipates, the tone changes dramatically. With the fugitives in handcuffs ("cuffs of love," as Dog calls them in one episode), disgust gives way to empathy.[42] Initially imagined as an animal ("tiger," "lot lizard," "wolf") or a monster ("wolf man," "Dracula"), the fugitive becomes a vulnerable human being ("girl," "kid"), a family member ("sister," "brother," "Dad," "daddy") or an equal ("brah," "friend," "man"). The Chapmans move from hunters to therapists, their prey from hardened criminals in need of punishment to troubled men and women in need of help. A punitive desire to degrade gives way to a therapeutic desire to transform. In the backseat of their SUV, Dog and Beth Chapman offer their captured fugitives cigarettes, ask them about their lives and their struggles with drugs, and give them hope of a future in which their spiritual, physical, and economic needs are met.

Family figures prominently in these backseat conversations. To convince offenders to sin no more, the Chapmans impress upon them their obligations to their kin, especially their children. In one episode, a fugitive named Tim gets into a shouting match with his girlfriend's mother, who is present at his apprehension. Dog intervenes by appealing to the man's love for his daughter: "How much do you love that baby girl?" Dog asks. "That's my world right there," Tim replies. "Then let's prove it, from this day, this second on." The family unit, the show insists, is the foundational source of economic security and social order. The implication is that love for family—in contrast to, say, living wage jobs—is the ultimate form of crime prevention. Tim, like most suspects, appears moved by the efforts made by the bounty hunters. He cries. He promises to change his ways ("I swear on my skin, everything," Tim says). And he thanks his captors for their kindness. "I should have listened to everyone from the start," he admits, demonstrating a submission to the moral order he had treated with contempt earlier in the episode. He is rewarded with hope. "You're getting rebuilt, refurbished, rehabilitated," Dog says to him.[43] After this counseling session, the Chapmans take their prisoner to jail and hand him over to the state.

Much of the power of these scenes comes from Dog's discussions of his own sinful past, which landed him in a Texas prison at the age of twenty-six for murder. Dog frequently shares, with fugitives and the show's audience, the story of his own transformation from wayward criminal to fatherly bounty hunter. In these scenes the show works to popularize what American Studies scholar Tanya Erzen has called the "testimonial politics" of evangelical Christians. With its emphasis on an individual decision to follow Jesus as the route to salvation, evangelicals have historically deployed testimonies, "narratives of sin, redemption, and personal transformation," that aim to convince listeners that God's grace extends to all who seek it. The testifier often confesses their own sinful past before describing a transformative experience in which they heard God's voice or felt his presence. In the late twentieth and early twenty-first centuries, Erzen notes, conservatives used testimony to justify the introduction of Christian laws and values into criminal justice policy.[44] The unspoken logic underlying testimonials is that government shouldn't be in the business of trying to make people into good citizens. Personal and social wellbeing requires a spiritual and familial grounding that the state can never provide. Dog's testimonies reflect this conservative ideology and aim for a similar rhetorical effect.

But the state does have a role to play. If the bounty hunter is the potter, the fugitive the clay, and the backseat testimonial-exhortation a kind of reshaping of the fugitive into a new form, jail is the kiln in which the fugitive's new self sets. It cannot be avoided. In one of his many testimonials, Dog explains that the experience of being stripped of individuality in prison can prompt a moral awakening:

> One of the things about going to prison is that you don't have a name anymore. You have a number. So it was the day I got my number and they said, "From now on you're no longer called the Dog. You're 271097." At that second, I said, "This is it. I'm now going to be the Dad that my Dad raised me to be."[45]

The experience of losing one's self, of becoming a number, Dog suggests, prompts an openness to change that previously did not exist. Ultimately, the degradation of incarceration is linked to a "tough love" approach to shaping behavior that has influenced everything from parenting guides to addiction treatment programs.[46] By accompanying the capture and caging of persons charged with crimes with a dose of testimonial politics, *Dog* spiritually justifies the violence visited upon these fugitives. Incarceration is represented as a constructive force rather than an act of deprivation that has devastating social, political, and economic effects on offenders and their families.

The show also masks the financially exploitative nature of bounty hunting. As bounty hunters the Chapmans are in an industry that scholars have argued places profits before justice. Judges who can outsource the cumbersome burden of monitoring people released on bail to private bondsmen have little fiscal incentive to avoid bail or consider defendants' "presumption of their innocence, their social and economic ties in the community, and the relatively minor nature of the alleged infraction."[47] Defendants who cannot afford to pay a percentage of their bail to a bondsman languish in jail. Those who can, meanwhile, remain under the control of the bounty hunter. As legal scholar Jonathan Drimmer explains, although bounty hunters "enjoy broader powers than police officers, they are unlicensed, unregulated, and generally free from constitutional constraints. They are legally entitled to break into a suspect's home without a warrant, arrest a suspect using necessary force, search and imprison suspects without prior authorization from the state."[48] By acting as slapdash therapists and on-the-fly social workers, the Chapmans challenge unflattering ideas of bounty hunters as mercenaries who exploit the poor. They become anti-authoritarian carriers of an authoritarian truth: the violence of incarceration is a necessary form of tough love. "Love" preempts more critical interpretations of the bounty hunters' violence as a fundamental element of a carceral state that uses the prison to manage economically superfluous, and thus threatening, populations.[49]

The show endears the Chapmans to viewers by presenting them as both morally righteous and slightly deviant. On one hand, the family appears to embody socially conservative fantasies of the nuclear family—patriarchal, grounded in traditional values, and, most significantly, evangelical Christian. A special Christmas episode offers an opportunity for Dog and Beth to expound upon their family values. Beth takes the girls into the kitchen to bake cookies. "It's very important that you girls keep this tradition going every Christmas, right? It brings me a lot of joy when I cook because I know it brings a lot of pleasure to so many in my family," she explains. Dog, meanwhile, stages an elaborate fake bounty hunt to capture Santa in order to convince his skeptical elementary school-age son Garry that Santa is real. "The Bible says that faith is the substance of things hoped for and the evidence of things not seen," Dog explains to the camera. "I got a chance to show Garry what faith is." The episode endorses traditional gender roles—women as carriers of the familial traditions that reinforce the importance of family, men as supervisors of their sons' journeys into manhood.[50]

In other moments, the family's righteousness manifests itself in the confident assertions that their work serves God. "It wasn't me that came [and] got you," Dog says to one captured fugitive. "It was the Lord sent me come get you."[51] Dog frequently invokes God, often in prayer circles led before and after bounty hunts. "Help us as we go out and capture this guy. . . . Help us find him and fix him," Dog says in one episode (fig. 6).[52] In one episode Dog meets a woman who cleaned up her act after he took

Figure 6. On *Dog the Bounty Hunter*, Duane "The Dog" Chapman leads his team in prayers before heading out on a hunt. Source: author screen capture.

her back to jail. Wendy, now a waitress, tells Dog, "I chose when I got out to start my life over. I'm just really happy to be sober and thank you guys for catching me." Dog says a prayer that thanks God for helping him to see, as he puts it, "that my work has made a difference in someone's life." Later, he says to the camera, "I just truly want to give. Sometimes I gotta get you down by the neck to accept it. But that's how I am."[53]

If cookie baking and "God is on our side" assertions were the totality of the Chapmans' image, they might appear rigid and unlikeable. But the show takes pains to show that the Chapmans' self-righteousness does not come at the expense of their humanity. Even as they rigorously voice their allegiance to a straight-and-narrow moral order, they remain lovingly imperfect, complex, playful, and contradictory. Dog's four marriages and his family's "postapocalyptic sense of fashion" do not fit the image of the wholesome evangelical Christian family that exists in the conservative imagination.[54] Dog and Beth express their sexuality in ways that would make moral traditionalists cringe. In one episode, for instance, Dog's son Leland mocks his tight-fitting, cheetah-print shirt. In response, Beth tells the camera, "They can make fun of their daddy all they want. I think that shirt's sexy. And at the end of the night it's me ripping that shirt off. So there."[55]

And while the show positively portrays the traditional gender socialization of the Chapman children, it also humorously depicts moments when Dog and Beth fail to live up to socially conservative ideals. Rather than being the Victorian voice of mercy and restraint, Beth is unabashedly less forgiving of the fugitives the family pursues. Dog "genuinely thinks there's good in everyone, however bad they may appear to be," she once told a reporter. "Whereas I just see them as bags of money with wings." That attitude appears often during the show. In one episode Dog has a change of heart about taking a suspect who has surrendered to jail. He believes the fugitive's claim that he missed his court appearance due to an honest mistake. "The just and merciful thing to do, because of his surrendering, is to let him walk," Dog says. Beth is irate. "So no macing? No action?" she asks indignantly.[56] She is also more vulgar in her interactions with the show's fugitives—especially the women. She calls a fugitive who had eluded capture a "nasty whore." When the fugitive is in custody, she initially refuses to try to counsel the woman before remanding her to the jail. "Doesn't want change, doesn't need help, doesn't need shit but jail," Beth vents.[57] Dog, meanwhile, is the more empathetic and forgiving of the two, unafraid to cry on camera and eager to speak about his own sinful past. He also enjoys housekeeping; we see him, in the first episode, vacuuming the family home. Such deviance from normative visions of gender and family renders the family's social conservatism more accessible to viewers raised in a culture that came to romanticize outsiders and embrace the aesthetics of rebellion.[58] The quasi-vigilante bonds that link these family members, the obviously blended nature of their family, and their mild subversion of our expectations (the hypermasculine Dog is the softie; the girly Beth has the foulest mouth of them all) make the Chapmans seem culturally credible.

In depicting its heroes as compassionate rebels and their antagonists as rebellious sinners, *Dog* reveals something about how punitiveness was popularized in the early twenty-first century. It did not always appeal to a vision of criminals as beasts or vermin who deserve nothing but scorn. In *Dog* popular messages about the criminal justice system seem aimed at satisfying a desire to see punishment as a generative, compassionate act. Criminals, *Dog* aimed to reassure its viewers, are not garbage to be thrown away. They can transcend their demons—addiction, self-hate, an internalized sense of impotence—and emerge from a period of suffering with a sense of self-possession.

The Problem of Hope

In 2011, on the 200th episode of *Dog the Bounty Hunter*, Duane Chapman reflected on the early days of shooting the show. He recalled being worried that his sympathy for those he captured would tank the show's ratings. "I was like, 'Oh my God. What are they going to think of me being nice to this criminal?' After the show was over, I looked down at the ground and thought, 'There goes my Hollywood chances—right out the window.' And lo and behold it became a hit."[59] Why, we might ask, *was* a show like *Dog*—with its surprisingly tender treatment of captured "bad guys"—popular? Why do other crimesploitation shows like *Lockup* and *Lockdown* similarly humanize those who are locked up? Two hundred years after Benjamin Rush's death, what accounts for the endurance of his long-disproven theory that the pains of degradation are spiritually regenerative for criminal offenders?

We suggest that a certain amount of optimism about offenders is required to make harsh punishment palatable to the public. In his study of why punishments change over time, cultural sociologist Philip Smith writes of a pattern. Forms of punishment flourish when the public perceives them as "eliminating the disgusting and unruly, effecting the decontamination of the spiritually and morally offensive, banishing evil, and enforcing cultural classifications and boundaries." Support for a punishment falters, conversely, when confidence in its ability to do these things declines. "When punishments put out more cultural pollution than they are deemed to eliminate, they are in trouble." Prisons, Smith notes, have been susceptible to charges that "the potentially virtuous [prisoners] were all too easily contaminated by contact with vice." Maximum-security facilities that separate and keep prisoners in their cells around the clock have also run into problems; they "have come in turn to be seen as factories of disorder churning out madmen and making unpredictable evil recidivists from petty criminals."[60] Nonetheless, the prison has never become so tainted in the public imagination that it was abolished. It has instead subsisted for over two centuries on a balance of pessimism and optimism—the darker assumptions about criminal incorrigibility tempered by the optimistic idea that prisons can be places where the wayward turn their lives around. Cynicism and hope work together to protect the prison's reputation as a punishment that controls, rather than contributes to, moral pollution.

Crimesploitation prison shows reflect and reinforce this balance of skepticism and hopefulness about incarcerated people. If they only depicted prisons as warehouses for the violent and the incorrigible, shows like *Dog*, *Lockup*, and *Lockdown* would risk undermining our most cherished ideas about humanity: that we are moral beings, endowed with the capacity to transcend our animality. The inclusion of stories of inmates growing and redeeming themselves and authorities showing care and compassion for those they cage work to ward off nihilistic feelings about the prison.

Hope also works on a psychological level. Numerous studies have measured the punitive response humans have toward people who have behaved unjustly. They have found that retribution—a desire to "get even"—motivates our desires to punish.[61] Our urge to punish wrongdoers persists even when punishment won't make us safer or happier.[62] But punishment *can* be satisfying, researchers suggest, when we receive feedback from the punished person that she has experienced a positive moral change in response to the punishment. When participants in one experiment punished fellow players of a game who had abused a position of advantage, one study found that the "satisfaction" they received from meting out the punishment was directly proportional to the degree to which the offender endorsed the moral message the punishment was trying to convey.[63] Hearing "I deserved this punishment" can make the punishment seem meaningful and worthwhile.

By offering audiences hope about the future of at least some of the people held in the nation's jails and prisons, crimesploitation may have made satisfying what otherwise might have come to seem pointless. A defining feature of the age of mass incarceration is not simply the magnitude of punishment, but its invisibility.[64] Those convicted of crime disappear shortly after their sentencing, sometimes forever, leaving the public with few options for observing whether the punishment has had any kind of moral effect on the criminal. In this context *Dog*, *Lockup*, and *Lockdown* offer a surrogate solution to this problem. Presenting stories of offenders responding morally and spiritually to their punishment, these shows may make the pain of punishment visible and meaningful, and thus satisfying, for viewers.

Such meaning is ultimately built on a lie that has been circulating through American culture since the Enlightenment. As Caleb Smith puts it, "more than any institution, the prison manifests the power of the law to disfigure and kill . . . in the name of humanity."[65] But degradation does not catalyze rehabilitation. Those who leave the prison are not elevated back into some noble humanity, but physically, politically, and socially disfigured by the experience. Yet the myth that dehumanization benefits prisoners persists. It haunts *Dog*'s backseat epiphanies. It underlies guards'—and sometimes prisoners'—on camera testimonials in *Lockup* about the spiritual benefits of being caged. That, in the end, is what makes this kind of crimesploitation particularly invidious. By appealing to viewers' progressive instincts, crimesploitation exploits its viewers as well as its subjects. In a world divided into good and evil, it manipulates the good "us" as well as the bad "them."

Challenging Spectatorship

What, we might ask, might documentary portrayals of the prison look like that unsettle these pernicious myths? One answer lies in the way prison documentaries situate the viewer in relationship to the experience of incarceration. In his broader exploration of documentary voice, media scholar Bill Nichols argues that documentaries aim to give audience members a sense that the film is addressing them as "socially situated viewers," speaking to them about a "common world" they share with the documentarian.[66] Sharing a common world, however, is not the same as being implicated in how it functions. Whether unsympathetically portraying the prison as a holding pen for dangerous predators or a place of moral rebirth for salvageable souls, prison crimesploitation fosters in its viewers a sense of social and ethical distance from what they see on screen. Prison becomes a necessary evil or a fact of (someone else's) life for which they bear no responsibility.

To unsettle the logic of the prison, then, portrayals of it must unveil the structural causes and effects of incarceration. They must show viewers how they are both affected by and responsible for human caging. And they must portray that caging as something other than a necessary evil or a positive good. One example is critical geographer Brett Story's 2016 documentary film *The Prison in Twelve Landscapes*. Consisting of twelve vignettes, the film depicts neither prisons nor prisoners but communities and spaces outside of prison that are affected by mass incarceration. As Story puts it,

> My hope is to make the prison a subject of reinvigorated debate, by suggesting that it operates not just as a building *over there*, but as a structure of power braided deeply into the relationships, economies and landscapes all around us. By upsetting expectations about

where prisons are to be found, the film attempts to destabilize our own assumed relationship to them; to pose new questions about the work that prisons do in our society and whether that work is necessary or desirable.[67]

The goal, she explains, is to "upend the commonsense understanding of prisons as indivisible from the problem of crime." In its place, she aims to show that the prison is not so much a building as it is a "set of relationships" that have little to do with actual threats to safety and much to do with the political economy of late capitalism: the management of surplus labor in a postindustrial economy, the reconfiguration of property relations in gentrifying cities, the construction of citizenship in ways that justify the contraction of the social safety net.[68] Each vignette highlights something the prison does to people and places *not* surrounded by barbed wire, from private security officers patrolling downtown Detroit's "opportunity zone" to a line of people waiting for a bus in midtown Manhattan that will take them upstate to visit their incarcerated loved ones.

Story's film works against prison crimesploitation, and specifically its "humanizing" dimensions that we have highlighted here. A common trope of prison documentaries is the portrayal of a sympathetic prisoner whose structural disadvantages are noted, yet who only earns sympathy by being "repentant for his crimes, which belong to him as 'bad choices' rather than policing prerogatives or judicial dictates."[69] Story counters that cliché by interviewing a woman who tells a harrowing story of spending four days in a jail cell for refusing to pay a ridiculous fine for a missing cover on her garbage bin. Then, refusing to allow that story to stand alone, Story takes her audience to the nearby municipal court in Florissant, Missouri where a line populated mostly by poor people of color snakes out the building and into the parking lot. They are there to pay or contest fines they have received for similar petty offenses—and to avoid the shackles that might be placed on them if those citations go unpaid. As the camera slowly pans down the line, the film powerfully suggests that the injustices of the neoliberal carceral state are best apprehended not in isolated stories of individuals making "choices," but as a foundational dimension of what *New York Times* columnist Thomas B. Edsall calls "poverty capitalism," in which "costs of essential government services are shifted to the poor."[70] In this framing, the prison is no longer a cage for animals or a site of rebirth for sinners, but a violent embodiment of our political and economic order. In this new way of seeing of the prison, Story explains, "the lines between the 'inside' and the 'outside' become blurred." The criminal justice system becomes "a set of social relations to which the audience members also belong, participate in, and bear responsibility for."[71]

4

Middlebrow Crimesploitation

"The 2010s was the decade that our collective interest in true crime boiled over into a full-on obsession," *Rolling Stone* astutely observed in late 2019.[1] Throughout the decade, a wave of serialized true crime documentaries had captured the nation's attention. A trio of "extra-judicial investigations" into unusual murder cases that police had resolved—*Making a Murderer* (Netflix), *The Jinx* (HBO), and the podcast *Serial* (NPR)—were so compelling that they became part of the story of these cases, prompting popular campaigns to reopen them. The runaway success of these programs inspired a proliferation of true crime docuseries. Unlike traditional true crime documentaries (which were feature-length films like Errol Morris's *The Thin Blue Line* [1988] or *Paradise Lost: The Child Murders at Robin Hood Hills* [1996]) or ordinary crimesploitation (which adopted the perspective of the authorities), these productions pioneered a new approach to engaging viewers in the spectacle of crime and punishment: an up-to-twenty-hour look at a single case, divided into episodes. In the years that followed, Netflix alone released *The Staircase* (2004/2018), *The Keepers* (2018), *Don't F**k with Cats: Hunting an Internet Killer* (2019), *Jeffrey Epstein: Filthy Rich* (2020), and *How to Fix a Drug Scandal* (2020).

With high production values and long running times, these productions presented themselves as a sophisticated alternative to crimesploitation, out to probe beneath surface-level appearances. Whereas familiar forms of crimesploitation often seem like "copaganda"—"more about order than about law"—these programs often adopted a critical stance toward the state.[2] Driven by an awareness that legal and political authorities are fallible, biased, and corruptible, they embraced what one scholar has called "the liberal-legal American model of law," which imagines the law as a crucial bulwark against the abuse of power by state actors. This approach to law holds sacred the presumption of innocence and criminal defendants' rights to due process; both are regarded as necessary checks on the government's power to punish suspected criminals even if the price we sometimes must pay for these goods is that "the innocent suffer while the guilty are able to capitalize upon their misdeeds."[3]

At first glance, then, these programs appear to offer a sophisticated alternative to crimesploitation, rejecting its sensational style and its preoccupation with the grotesque, the scandalous, and the lascivious. Yet we argue that many of these explorations of criminal justice in the United States are better understood as a middlebrow form of crimesploitation, delivering lowbrow thrills under a veneer of intellectual heft and high-minded critique.[4] Indeed, like its lowbrow counterparts, middlebrow crimesploitation presents its stories using the conventions of melodrama. It divides the world into good and evil, heroes and villains. It dwells on threats to those who are innocent and powerless, sometimes indulging viewers' fantasies of vanquishing those threats and rescuing the innocent. And it "speaks to widely frustrated desires for some secure measure of control over one's own circumstances and conditions of existence" in a world in which "vulnerability is a condition that runs rampant."[5]

Middlebrow crimesploitation only seems different because it inverts the familiar dynamics of crimesploitation to achieve many of the same pleasures. In shows like *Cops*, *To Catch a Predator*, and *Lockup*, as we have seen, criminals are presented as the source of insecurity in the world, authorities as the antidote to it, and viewers as responsible citizens who have important, surveillance-oriented roles to play in assisting authorities. In middlebrow productions, by contrast, this dynamic is frequently inverted. Tapping into themes found in other corners of tabloid culture, like daytime talk shows, these programs cater to "popular dissatisfaction with institutions perceived as incapable of fulfilling the great promises of liberal democracy."[6] Viewers of these programs become jurors in "alternative trials" produced by the documentarians, whose own ingenuity and skepticism brings to light incompetence, ignorance, and illogic that pervaded the actual trial.[7] These programs thus invite skepticism of the state's capacity to find and validate the truth. Viewers are not so much deputized *by* the state as they are deputized *against* it; their participatory impulses are channeled toward evaluating, criticizing, and revising the conclusions reached by authorities in criminal cases.

In what follows, we argue that the critical orientation of many of these programs is superficial. We take as our case studies three programs released by Netflix in recent years: *Making a Murderer* (2015), *How to Fix a Drug Scandal* (2020), and *Don't F**k with Cats* (2019). We argue that, in crucial ways, these series fail to achieve the goal of critiquing the substance and structure of the criminal justice system and the bigger picture of hegemonic power relations in the United States that supports it. While they may sow skepticism about police and prosecutorial power and extol the importance of values like due process and the presumption of innocence, they ultimately do little to encourage a deeper interrogation of the criminal justice system and the politics that have made the United States a punitive outlier among western democracies.[8] Moreover, the genre frequently invites viewers to become investigators who solve criminal cases that the state has ignored or, as a result of incompetence or corruption, botched. These shows offer viewers quasi-vigilante pleasures by inviting them to drop in and play around in other people's worst nightmares. One household's trauma—the murder of a child, the wrongful incarceration of a father—becomes another household's Friday night Netflix binge.

Making a Murderer, the "Innocence Revolution," and the Middlebrow Imagination

Toward the end of the 2016 holiday season, over 19 million Netflix viewers became captivated by the story of Steven Avery. In 2005 authorities in Manitowoc County, Wisconsin charged Avery and his nephew Brendan Dassey with the murder of Teresa Halbach, a photographer for *AutoTrader Magazine* who disappeared after visiting Avery's property to photograph a vehicle. Avery's case was notable because those same authorities had wrongfully convicted him of sexually assaulting and savagely beating Penny Ann Beernsten in Manitowoc County in 1985. After serving eighteen years of a thirty-five-year sentence, Avery had been exonerated and freed by DNA evidence in 2003. The documentary tells the story of his initial conviction and exoneration before probing the merits of the new murder charge. The filmmakers explore evidence pointing toward guilt or innocence for Avery and Dassey, who prosecutors alleged participated in the murder.

Making a Murderer takes seriously the possibility that county officials conspired to turn Halbach's murder into an opportunity to punish Avery for the reputational hit the government took in the aftermath of his exoneration and the lawsuit he subsequently filed against the county. The filmmakers focus on the defense's theory that county officials conspired to frame Avery for the murder. They scrutinize the actions of county officials, revealing everything from problems in the chain of custody of forensic evidence to the improper involvement of investigators with a conflict of interest. In their depiction of Avery's nephew, Dassey, moreover, the filmmakers suggest that the collateral damage of the county's corruption was the mistreatment and conviction of an innocent sixteen-year-old boy. As galling as the problems they uncover in Avery's case is their depiction of investigators' interrogation of Dassey. Taking advantage of Dassey's limited cognitive capacities, the police, and then, shockingly, an investigator working for his own court-appointed defense attorney coerced an incoherent and implausible confession from the teenager. Despite the glaring flaws in the prosecution's cases against them, juries ultimately convicted Avery and Dassey of the murder, and the final episodes of the series examine the aftermath: Avery's return to a prison system that unjustly held him for eighteen years and Dassey's prospects for a new trial.

In contrast to lowbrow forms of crimesploitation, *Making a Murderer* unapologetically embraces the importance of the rights and vigorous defense of those accused of crime. Indeed, the onscreen consciences of the docuseries are Avery's defense attorneys, Jerome Buting and Dean Strang. Privately hired with funds Avery had received in a settlement with the county, the two attorneys leave no stone unturned in their efforts to hold the prosecution to its burden of proof. We see them not only thoroughly examining and criticizing each piece of evidence proffered by the state, but also objecting on technical grounds to prosecutorial tactics at trial. In their hands, rights become a sacred good. Because the docuseries cultivates doubt about the integrity of the police investigation, the right to counsel, the right to confront witnesses, and the right to exhaustive discovery, process becomes a potential lifesaver. With its apparent preference for process over outcome, *Making a Murderer* marks itself as different from the presumption of guilt and desire for on-the-spot justice shows like *Cops* and *To Catch a Predator* reinforce.

Ultimately, however, the show undercuts its liberal-legal call for sober-minded, rule-bound administration of justice by neutral third parties. For filmmakers Demos and Ricciardi, the value of defendants' rights lies not in the protection they provide to the innocent and guilty alike, but in the power they give to the innocent to combat unjust punishment. A remark made by one of Avery's attorneys in the show's final episode captures this sentiment. Dean Strang says that he "almost hopes Steve is guilty" because the prospect of his twice suffering wrongful conviction is too overwhelming to bear.[9] Strang's comments illustrate how innocence can overshadow the liberal-legal value of protecting defendants' constitutional rights for their own sake. The protection of factually innocent people from the devastation of incarceration becomes the most pressing criminal justice policy imperative, leaving untouched the question of why such a devastating punishment is so easily and readily meted out.

Indeed, in its focus on the question of Avery's and Dassey's guilt or innocence (which the producers oddly claimed was not the point of the series), *Making a Murderer* limits the scope of its engagement with the criminal justice system.[10] Like other middlebrow crimesploitation "Whodunnits," the show capitalized upon the several decades of DNA-based exonerations of wrongfully convicted persons. As awareness of the problem of wrongful conviction rose in the 2000s, Americans became increasingly sensitive to how often and easily their criminal justice systems can produce unjust outcomes. This focus on the conviction of the innocent for terrible crimes, in turn, could foster a kind of myopia. As terrible as they are, wrongful convictions are but one form of injustice that plagues the most punitive nation in the world. Critics, though, have noted the limits of criminal justice reform efforts that revolve around the problem of wrongful conviction.[11] Legal scholar Robert J. Norris argues that the innocence movement is best viewed *not* as a "new civil rights movement," but rather a "relatively small but intensely powerful piece of other modern civil rights struggles."[12] Criminal justice reform efforts that focus on avoiding the wrongful conviction of the innocent risk diverting the public's attention away from other struggles, like ending the criminalization and surveillance of Black youth, ensuring the quality of defense lawyers for the indigent, or curbing prosecutors' practice of overcharging defendants in order to induce guilty pleas in sentencing deals.[13] And it ignores altogether the conditions of incarceration and the enormous barriers that exist for inmates who attempt to challenge inhumane treatment and conditions.[14]

The show's focus on a conspiracy theory—that Avery and Dassey were framed by the police—does not just divert attention away from the more widespread forms of injustice that plague the administration of criminal justice in the United States. It also provides the perfect story with which to deliver the sensational thrills that makes run-of-the-mill crimesploitation so popular. On its surface, *Making a Murderer* presents itself as a critic of media that aims to manipulate viewers' emotions and cater to their lurid tastes. In one episode the filmmakers present with critical detachment footage of a *Dateline* NBC reporter speaking candidly to them about the news business. "Right now, murder is hot, it's what everyone wants, it's what the competition wants," she admits. "We're trying to get the perfect murder story." By turning a critical eye on exploitative media coverage of the case, *Making a Murderer* invites disdain for a news media that commodifies traumatic events. One of the series's most emotionally intense scenes captures Barbara Tadych—Brendan Dassey's mother—storming out of the courthouse after her son is found guilty only to be accosted by television journalists trying to document her reaction. Her husband, Scott Tadych, yells at the camera-operators and journalists nearby, "Get the fuck out of here! Leave her alone! Get the fuck out of here!" This scene is constructed so that the viewers are positioned at a critical distance from the crowd of media vultures surrounding Dassey's distraught relatives.

But for all its handwringing about media sensationalism, the docu-series adopts a fundamentally melodramatic approach to its subject matter that is frequently found in tabloid culture. Melodramas are stories told in a "mode of excess."[15] A surfeit of sentimental detail infuses characters, settings, and events with a heightened emotionality. In a typical melodramatic plot, evil, one-dimensional antagonists try to bring ruin upon equally one-dimensional heroes or heroines who are wholly good and innocent. While casting *Dateline* and other news media as sensationalist tabloids, *Making a Murderer* caters to its own audiences' desires to consume three classical elements of melodrama: powerlessness transcended, evil vanquished, and shocking secrets revealed.

Damsels in Distress, Powerlessness, and Rescue

Melodramas traffic in moral binaries. Dark-hatted evildoers prey upon vulnerable protagonists, like the classic damsels in distress tied to railroad tracks. *Making a Murderer* offers a variation on this trope. It does not adopt a vision of the Avery family as the carriers of unadulterated goodness and virtue, but it does depict the family as powerless and naïve.

Throughout the series, a recurring shot periodically fills the screen that depicts the family's vulnerability.[16] The camera pans down the rows upon rows of junked cars that sustain the family's auto-salvaging business, reminding the audience that the Avery family literally lives in a junkyard (fig. 7). Those junk-filled establishing shots punctuate scenes in the series that reinforce common stereotypes of poor white people as "trash."[17] Bad hygiene is one. Avery's appellate lawyer for his first case explains that part of the government's evidence did not make sense because "the victim identified the perpetrator as wearing white underwear when Steve Avery did not even own underwear." Chemical dependency is another. Chuck Avery (Steven's brother) and Jodi Stachowski (Steven's fiancé) are almost always smoking cigarettes, a depiction that taps into popular constructions of lower-class smokers as failed citizens self-medicating in the face of poverty and exclusion. A lack of shame is a third. A bizarre scene near the end of the series features Allan Avery (Steven's father) wandering around an overgrown garden and ruminating about his son's fate and the herbs he is growing. It ends with him impulsively plucking a piece of lettuce and stuffing it in his mouth, utterly unconcerned with the unseemliness of casually eating in the middle of an on-camera interview (fig. 8).

It is tempting to write off the filmmakers' depiction of the family as "poverty porn," a term used by communication scholars to denote any depiction of the poor that "appeals to an ignoble audience interest, is patronizing and reductionist, robs its subjects of their dignity, and ignores systemic failings."[18] And yet the show also romanticizes the Avery family at times, indulging in a cultural tendency to imagine "people living on the margins, without economic or political or social privilege, as possessing something vital, some essential quality that had somehow been lost from" the lives of middle-class people.[19] Just as classical melodramas portrayed rural folk as carriers of a bygone goodness in a decadent, cosmopolitan world, *Making a Murderer* portrays the Avery family as unrefined and naïve, yet uncommonly loyal and loving. Nothing, the docuseries suggests, will stop them from standing by Steven and Brendan and doing all they can to bring the two home. Indeed, it is because they are unconcerned with appearances or privacy that viewers are able to witness the depth of their loyalty to one another. In these moments, reductionist portrayals of the Avery family as poor whites make them worthy of admiration.

The depiction of the Avery family's lack of social and cultural capital sets up the sense of relief that the filmmakers invite the audience to feel when

Figure 7. The Avery family home is a junkyard on *Making a Murderer*. Source: author screen capture.

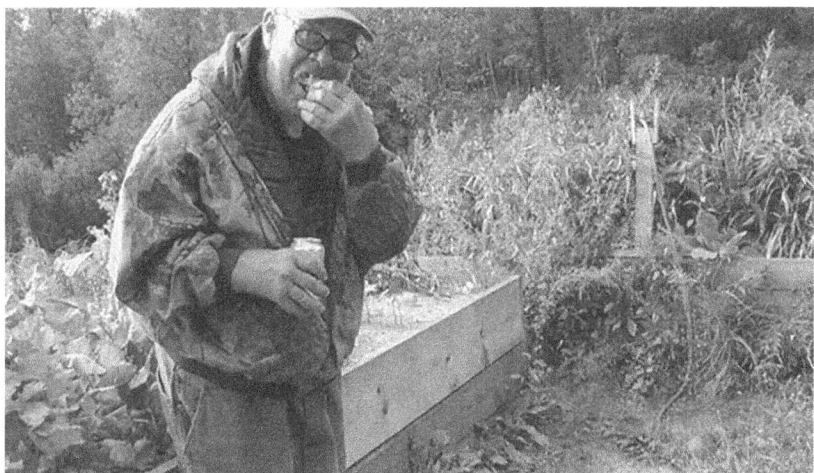

Figure 8. Allen Avery eats lettuce in his garden while being interviewed on *Making a Murderer*. Source: author screen capture.

Steven Avery's defense attorneys arrive on the scene. Jerome Buting and Dean Strang save the family from abject defeat by putting up a formidable fight on Avery's behalf. In a modern variation on a classic melodramatic plot, they emerge as the heroes who untie Avery from the railroad tracks as a train conducted by a corrupt prosecutor barrels toward him. The problem with this rendering is that it distorts the reality that most criminal defendants are indigent and never get rescued by defense attorneys with lavish amounts of time and resources to protect them from black-hatted prosecutors. It also fails to call attention to the nearly unchecked power prosecutors have in the United States. Prosecutors may bear the burden of proof in a criminal trial, but their charging discretion allows them to avoid trial in the vast majority of cases. By agreeing to drop or downgrade charges, they are able to negotiate plea deals in the vast majority of criminal cases. Most defendants in Avery's position face, as he once did, a criminal justice system in which due process is a cursory frame instead of a constantly insisted-upon value. By constructing a "social justice" film about the criminal justice system that revolves around the trial of a poor man, Demos and Ricciardi neglect the fact that trials, and the opportunity they afford defendants to ask their peers to evaluate the government's case against them, are rare events reserved for the privileged or those willing to risk spending years of their lives in cages if they lose.

The Degradation of Folk Devils

In *Making a Murder* state actors, rather than defendants, are depicted as the bad guys. And the baddest guy of all is Avery's prosecutor, Ken Kratz, whose integrity is called into question early in the series. The filmmakers depict him presiding over a press conference after Brenden Dassey confessed to investigators that he had participated with his uncle Steven in the rape and murder of Teresa Halbach. With barely controlled enthusiasm, he regales reporters with the story of the crime. The tale he tells is chock-full of images of sadomasochism and sexual violence. Kratz explains that Avery and Dassey chained Halbach to a bed and disemboweled her. Later, we learn facts that cast obvious doubt on Dassey's confession and see firsthand the coercive techniques that investigators used on the boy. We learn that no forensic evidence exists to support the story of torture and dismemberment he was led to tell. Ignoring the lack of any corroborating evidence to support the confession, and unconcerned with the effects that his hastily assembled press conference might have on potential jurors, Kratz visibly revels in this self-serving, extralegal moment of triumph over Avery.

Depictions of Kratz's prosecutorial recklessness set up the sense of schadenfreude that *Making a Murderer* invites audiences to feel when Kratz's personal and professional lives later collapse. Shortly after the conclusion of the cases, audiences learn, Kratz was sued by several women for sexual harassment, fired, and went into treatment for sex and drug addiction and narcissistic personality disorder. With clips of local news stories about Kratz's fall from grace, the show offers viewers the chance to pleasurably consume a punitive spectacle of a prosecutor's downfall. By placing a prosecutor in the position of degradation normally reserved for criminal defendants in lowbrow crimesploitation, *Making a Murderer* reveals the politically promiscuous appeal of humiliating retribution in contemporary American culture. With a kind of enlightened self-righteousness, the show incites the very retrograde emotions that have long buttressed the criminal justice system.

Shocking Revelations

Finally, *Making a Murderer* features melodramatic moments of revelation that invite responses of shock from viewers. A cliffhanger ending to the fourth episode of the series involves the discovery of evidence that appears to have been improperly handled by authorities. Having obtained a warrant to inspect the contents of the state's 1985 case file on Steven Avery, defense attorney Jerome Buting stands in a room with a special prosecutor and investigator and inspects a box containing a blood sample drawn from Avery during the investigation phase of his 1980s rape case. The camera zooms in on the edges of the box, revealing that a piece of tape has been used to reclose the seal. A Styrofoam container inside the box also appears as if it has been unsealed and resealed. The camera lingers on these close-up shots of the broken seals, inviting the viewer to inspect and evaluate the break in a piece of red tape marked "EVIDENCE." Finally, within that container, the clerk finds a test tube of blood. Its seal is also punctured. As the vial of blood is displayed to the camera, Buting is on the phone recapping the events he has just witnessed to his legal partner: "Get this . . . right in the center of the top of the tube is a little tiny hole, just about the size of a hypodermic needle." A muffled exclamation of surprise is heard coming through the cellphone. "And," Buting adds, "I spoke with a Labcorp person already who told me they don't do that." As a whoop is heard through his receiver, Buting asks,

> Have you fallen on the floor yet or no? Think about it, Dean. If Labcorp didn't stick a needle through that top, then who did? Some officer went into the file, opened it up, took a sample of Steven Avery's blood, and planted it in the Rav 4. Yeah, he knows where we're going. Game on. Exactly. Game on.[20]

The screen quickly cuts to the credits as uptempo rockabilly music plays— an adrenaline-pumping response to Buting's "game on."[21]

Collectively, these melodramatic elements of *Making a Murderer* obscure the systemic, structural, and depersonalized way in which the state's violence is often unjustly levied against those accused of crime. In interviews they gave to the press after the runaway success of the series, Demos and Ricciardi insisted that they had created "a social justice documentary" that "offered a window into the system."[22] But, as we have shown, systemic analysis is upstaged by the show's substantive focus and melodramatic framing. In the world of *Making a Murderer*, it is not unchecked prosecutorial discretion and the American politicization of the figure of the district attorney that is the problem. It is Ken Kratz's smug grandstanding. It is not overcrowded dockets, underfunded budgets for indigent defense, and the political pressure placed on law enforcement to clear cases that lead to wrongful convictions. It is the scarcity of heroic lawyers like Strang and Buting who can so effectively stand up to the government. Finally, it is not the normalization of harsh, punitive sentiment that is the problem. Nor is it the desire to degrade. It is instead the misdirection of those feelings toward innocent people.

The Punitive Defense of Liberal Legalism: A Case Study in Viewer Response

One (admittedly anecdotal) audience response to *Making a Murderer* illustrates how these melodramatic qualities—powerlessness and rescue, good guys versus bad guys, and shocking "gotcha" moments—can reinforce or maintain the conditions of harsh punishment even as the series purports to criticize the state. The most popular (or "up voted") discussion thread about the show on Reddit, one of the largest general-interest discussion communities on the Internet, shows how some audience members embraced the production's punitive subtext.[23] Rather than prompting criticism of the criminal justice system, the series elicited for some viewers a reverence for due process and defendants' rights that quickly morphed into a distinctive kind of illiberal punitiveness and vigilante desire to get involved in the criminal justice system that we have seen is common in crimesploitation.

The discussion began with the post, "Can we pause to applaud two of the best lawyers in the USA? Their sincerity was remarkable. Dean Strang and Jerome Buting are my first call if I get framed for murder." Announcing that he or she was going to play the role of devil's advocate, one viewer asked other Reddit community members to imagine the feelings that the victim's family must have had about Avery's attorneys. "These guys would seem pretty villainous," the viewer suggested. "Have you ever followed one of those cases where the proverbial smoking gun evidence is disallowed based on a technicality pointed out by the defense lawyer?" the viewer asked. "It's aggravating to watch someone work to set a seemingly guilty person free."[24]

A conversation about the value of criminal defense attorneys ensued. Redditors extolled the value of defense counsel as figures who keep the state honest. Even in cases of clear guilt, discussion participants suggested, it is important to ensure that the state meets its burden of proof and operates in a transparent, fair manner. One contributor to the discussion wrote that Steven Avery

> had the right to a fair trial in a justice system free from corruption . . . even if he is guilty. Facilitating this noble pursuit is the function of a criminal defense attorney. Strang and Buting couldn't be categorized as villainous even if Steve Avery had the undigested remains of [the victim] in his belly. Welcome to America.[25]

Even if Avery were guilty, another wrote,

> it is the duty of the attorney to defend his client with the goal of setting him/her free. Without this duty, without the presumption of innocence, without the right to a fair trial, we'd all be getting 'Avery'd' by the system.[26]

Another viewer, who identified himself as a criminal defense attorney, wrote.

> You have all these other rights in order to protect you from the government, who has an enormous wealth of resources compared

to an individual person. These rights belong to the guilty just as much as the innocently accused and we defense attorneys use them because if the police are allowed to bypass these rules, who's to say [they] will not violate the constitutional rights of an innocent?[27]

But the procedural understanding of justice that is at the heart of this romanticized portrayal of the legal system has not prevented the inhumane treatment of the guilty. Naomi Murakawa has argued that the prison population boom in the United States since the 1970s was largely built by, rather than in spite of, liberal legislators who saw the rights afforded by due process as adequate protections of human dignity in the criminal justice system. The result was a dressing up, rather than a reining in, of the state's use of violence to punish crime. With its power limited more by procedures than substantive values, the state could engage in nearly "limitless violence" against those convicted of crimes.[28] Just as the wrongful conviction movement privileges innocence over constitutional rights *per se*, Redditors' embrace of defense attorneys does nothing to limit the state's violence against the legally and factually guilty. The celebration of a liberal-legal model of American law that *Making a Murderer* stoked is, in the end, a diversion from the contemplation of what political scientist Marie Gottschalk has called the "wider question of what constitutes justice for the guilty."[29]

Indeed, the discussion shows how easily the defense of due process can coexist with a zeal for punishment. Responding to the good-versus-evil binary that the docuseries constructed, viewers relived an exchange in which Avery's attorneys one-upped the prosecution. A courtroom disagreement about the prosecution's plans to capitalize upon Brendan Dassey's alleged confession led defense attorney Strang to rehearse, in open court, the presumption of innocence, saying,

> All due respect to counsel, the State is supposed to start every criminal case swimming upstream. And the strong current against which the State is supposed to be swimming is a presumption of innocence. That presumption of innocence has been eroded, if not eliminated, here by the specter of [the co-conspirator].[30]

Remembering that moment, one commentator on Reddit wrote,

> I was tickled to death when he said that. I felt like a kid watching Wrestle Mania VII where Sgt. Slaughter tried to pin Hogan with

the Iraq flag and Hogan jumps up all bloody at the last second and takes him out with a leg drop. That's pretty much how Strang handled [prosecutor Ken] Kratz on this exchange.

Another wrote, "These men were batman. Trying to fight the good fight in the face of a corrupt Gotham city. The heroes we need but don't deserve." And a third wrote,

> I don't normally imagine a "defense attorney" as being an Ayn Rand style Conservative, but I saw Strang & Buting as believers in freedom, and the truth no matter what. It really struck me that they saw government desire driving the case vs the facts and fought it as [best] they could."[31]

Instead of tempering the will to punish that is so common in the crimesploitation we have discussed in earlier chapters, the middlebrow *Making a Murderer* simply redirects it, for these viewers, against a loathed prosecutor. The series serves as a reminder that punitivism is not only a conservative, reactionary phenomenon. For different reasons and in the service of different ends, progressives and liberals have embraced punitive responses to social problems. When left-wing and libertarian critiques of state punishment rejoice at the downfall of punitive bad guys, they risk reinforcing the emotional foundations of the neoliberal carceral state they aim to disrupt.

By demonizing figures like Ken Kratz, moreover, the film makes it harder to see the need for systemic reform. There is little doubt that Ricciardi and Demos hoped that their film would increase public awareness about systemic problems in the criminal justice system and spur reforms aimed at remediating those problems. But by casting individuals, rather than structures and systems, as the source of all the injustice we see, the two made the problem seem case-specific and narrow. Viewers responded accordingly. Outraged by what they saw, over 100,000 people signed a petition asking President Obama to pardon Steven Avery (a power he did not have, given the case's prosecution in a state court).[32] Guided by a program that did not situate the Avery case in a larger context, audiences responded to the injustice they perceived by demanding executive clemency in a singular case rather than proposing a broader, federal action aimed at curbing unbridled prosecutorial discretion or abusive interrogation techniques.

The Pleasures of Sleuthing

At the heart of the appeal of *Making a Murderer* and many of the true crime docuseries of the 2010s is an appeal to the joy of solving mysteries. In productions like *Serial, The Jinx, The Staircase,* and *The Keepers,* the documentarian identifies a crime, usually with bizarre circumstances, presents the crime as a mystery that the documentary is trying to get to the bottom of, and sutures the viewer into the narrative as a juror who evaluates the existing case against a defendant or a "co-sleuth" who investigates alternative theories of the crime.[33] As Sheila Nevins, HBO's head of documentary programming said,

> Shows like *The Jinx* give the audience a sense of value to know that they can help bring justice. They become the jury, and that's an investment that very often passive TV can't make. I think the magic of true crime is when you are getting someone out or putting someone in prison. You are part of a jury. You are actively engaged in making a decision.[34]

Often these programs begin by asking the question: Who committed this crime? They then call the existing answers to those questions into doubt, showing how they are too simplistic, potentially clouded by bias and political self-interest, and at odds with knowledge or evidence that has been ignored. The filmmakers or on-screen surrogates for the narrative position of investigator use forensic or pseudo-forensic techniques to unravel the mystery, undermine the authorities' claim about who the criminal is, or both.

As a result of its innate distrust of appearances, middlebrow crimesploitation overlaps, in many ways, with the mystery genre. In his treatise on the appeal of the mystery as a literary genre philosopher Alan H. Goldman provides a useful summary of scholars' explanations of the appeal of the detective novel:

> Mystery fiction provides relaxation through intellectual games or puzzles much like crosswords or like magic tricks when the puzzles cannot be solved. It relieves anxiety by showing that justice prevails. It provides an exciting escape from humdrum reality. It exhibits narrative purity and intelligibility, having fully coherent stories with clear beginnings and closure at endings, in contrast to other modern fiction. It affirms the power of reason, symbolizing the

knowability and lawlike nature of the world, the existence of hard facts, and the power of scientific reasoning or inductive inference, ubiquitous in mental life but clearly exhibited here. It bridges the gap between obscure scientific method and the layman, showing that the former can serve moral purposes. It legitimates and reaffirms the values of the status quo or privileged class by segregating the criminal, at the same time exorcising guilt from upper-class readers. And it provides a vicarious outlet for violent, homicidal, or sadistic impulses, stimulating voyeurism of the criminal class.[35]

Building on these explanations, Goldman proposes that mystery appeals to consumers because it invites them to become sleuths alongside the narrative's detective, piecing together the clues of the mystery. But its appeal also lies, he argues, in its invitation to "think like the criminal." The epistemological pleasures culminate in satisfaction—an unambiguous factual and moral resolution.[36]

Middlebrow crimesploitation often serves up similar pleasures—to a point. It sets up a mystery with real-life illicit details and serious consequences. It taps into our desires to know, by the end, that *this* person killed Teresa Halbach, or *this* person framed Steven Avery, or—in its most nuanced version—*this* part of the system failed. And it enlists viewers as investigators, trying to discover the truth alongside the narratives' "detectives"—offscreen figures like the documentary's producers or onscreen ones like Dean Strang (*Making a Murderer*). But because it is tethered to a world in which the endings are determined by official institutions—courts and police agencies—middlebrow crimesploitation only sometimes wraps up tidily with an unambiguous answer to the questions it pursues. Often its resolution lies not in offering closure, but in demonstrating that the closure that has been achieved by official institutions is false or built on fraudulent practices.

Putting the Government on Trial

A different kind of co-sleuthing can be found in the 2020 Netflix production *How to Fix a Drug Scandal*. This serial explores two scandalous crimes by individual laboratory technicians in two state-run forensic laboratories in Massachusetts, one in Amherst and the other in Boston. Each technician was arrested; one in 2012 and the other in 2013. In Amherst lab technician Sonja Farak started consuming methamphetamine and cocaine collected by police for evidence, quickly developing a serious addiction that led her to nine years of stealing and using those drugs. In Boston lab technician Annie Dookhan falsified lab reports that were used to convict defendants in drug crime cases over a span of eight years.[37] In each situation, the consequences of each individual's misconduct turned out to be considerable, leading to the dismissal of thousands of convictions.[38] Prosecutors working at the state's Attorney General office, meanwhile, opposed efforts to vacate the convictions of those defendants whose cases were handled by these two lab technicians. Even worse, in Farak's case, they misled the court and did not turn over exculpatory evidence to the defense attorneys. That evidence revealed that Farak's on-the-job drug use had begun in 2004 rather than 2012—affecting thousands more cases than those the court initially assumed were tainted. The scandals were unrelated except that they took place in the same state around the same time. Unlike *Making a Murderer*, the program is not a whodunit but a "why did this happen?" The show alternates between Amherst and Boston, following timelines of the misconduct of Farak and Dookhan, developing parallel narratives of governmental dysfunction.

Unlike traditional crimesploitation fare, the serial blames the injustice it depicts on meso-level institutional failure rather than the moral deficiencies of individuals.[39] Farak and Dookhan—and, for that matter, prosecutors who resisted the defense attorneys' efforts to reveal the true scope of the scandal—are not villainized. Early in the series, one of the attorneys, Luke Ryan, explains to the camera how his perspective on criminal justice differs from that of prosecutors:

> The search for truth that happens in criminal cases on the prosecution side is a search for truth for a very narrow period of time. . . . [Prosecutors] want to know what happened in the exact moment that a crime was committed, and they really don't care at all about what happened to defendants up to that moment that caused them to be in that position where they made those choices. And I realized that the work of criminal defense attorneys often is about [calling attention to] the way in which systems fail people and create environments where these choices end up happening.[40]

He goes on to point out that a focus on systems rather than evildoers is "a truth that's unpopular, and people don't like to hear about it."[41] By framing the defense attorneys as the heroes of the story, the series adopts—for the most part—this perspective. The two corrupt lab technicians are depicted mostly as troubled but sympathetic characters whose misbehavior nevertheless caused profound trouble for many drug crime defendants in Massachusetts and consequently illuminated institutional oversight problems in the state's legal system. And unlike *Making a Murderer*, the Massachusetts prosecutors are collectively, rather than individually, castigated. *How to Fix a Drug Scandal* suggests that their behavior is a product of institutional structures that lack the safeguards needed to keep government actors honest. Human weakness, rather than evil, is the source of the problem. As another defense attorney, Daniel Marx, explains, "I don't like to demonize people. I think good people give into bad impulses. I think people want to avoid work. They want to avoid embarrassment. They want to avoid losing cases."[42]

There may not be any villains in *How to Fix a Drug Scandal*, but there are heroes: justice prevails because dogged underdog defense attorneys listened to their gut. The celebration of their underdog heroism, however, replaces what might have been calls for radical institutional change. Reflecting on these cases in the final moments of the last episode in the series, *Boston Globe* reporter Scott Allen tells viewers that the scandals

> showed us a lot of things that people take for granted. The machinery of justice, the people who make it work—they're not benign. They're not neutral, necessarily. If we don't insist on it, then they won't be fair and impartial. Watching this unfold has taught me a lot about the role of defense attorneys in the legal system, and how they keep prosecutors accountable. Because what ultimately brought this all to light was a lot of very, very relentless attorneys, filing motion after motion, getting denied over and over and over again for years, seemingly knowing in their gut that something had gone wrong.[43]

The systemic problems the series flags are numerous. Severely underfunded drug laboratories are pressure cookers that lack oversight and encourage cutting corners. The state's chemists lack professional independence; they grow loyal to prosecutors with whom they work, encouraging them to be biased against defendants. Prosecutors have inordinate discretion, and they sometimes use it to protect their own interests rather than to seek justice.[44] But rather than calling for radical changes that would remedy these problems institutionally, the series lapses into a celebration of an adversarial legal system, ultimately promoting the retention of the status quo.[45] With a little luck and enough tenacity, the show suggests, public defenders can hold prosecutors accountable and ensure that justice is served.

How to Fix a Drug Scandal is important because it reveals how middlebrow crime docuseries exist on a spectrum, with some closer to the lowbrow crimesploitation we have spent much of this book exploring and others closer to critical documentaries like Brett Story's *The Prison in Twelve Landscapes* that we discussed in chapter 3. Neither a critical documentary nor lowbrow "trash," *How to Fix a Drug Scandal* falls somewhere between the two poles. Like other series of its ilk, it has moments of critical potential. By exploring and criticizing the failures of state bureaucracies—in particular, the Massachusetts procuracy and courts system—the series attends to institutional structures in ways that crimesploitation in its purest form does not. And to its credit, the series mostly avoids fetishizing the "takedown" of a morally reprehensible individual (though it does show us prosecutors squirming on the stand when they finally face accusations of misconduct). There is no equivalent to Ken Kratz in this story.[46]

But *How to Fix a Drug Scandal* ultimately stays at the meso-level—focusing on parts of one criminal justice system in one American state. Missing is the connection of this single state's experience with a broader history of lax accountability and poor conditions in forensic labs across the nation. Scandals have happened in crime labs across the nation's large and small jurisdictions, from revelations in 2002 that the Houston crime lab was afflicted with "water leaks that destroyed evidence" and deliberate misconduct by "unqualified criminalists" to the discovery in 2015 that a crime lab technician in Bend, Oregon, had tampered with evidence in as many as 1,100 cases.[47] In 2009, the National Academy of Sciences released a report on the state of forensic science in the United States in which it identified a troubling lack of national or state standards for crime laboratories:

> Operational principles and procedures for many forensic science disciplines are not standardized or embraced, either between or within disciplines. There is no uniformity in the certification of forensic practitioners, or in the accreditation of crime laboratories. Indeed, most jurisdictions do not require forensic practitioners to be certified, and most forensic science disciplines have no mandatory certification programs. . . . Often there are no standard protocols governing forensic practice in a given discipline. And,

even when protocols are in place . . . they often are vague and not enforced in any meaningful way. . . . These shortcomings obviously pose a continuing and serious threat to the quality and credibility of forensic science practice.[48]

In 2013 President Barack Obama created a National Commission on Forensic Science to propose remedies to these problems, including "guidelines on how to retain evidence and on security procedures in crime labs."[49] Shortly after Donald Trump's inauguration, Attorney General Jeff Sessions disbanded the commission before its work was finished. *How to Fix a Drug Scandal* makes no note of this recent history. Indeed, in calling what happened in Massachusetts a "scandal," singular, the series makes the events it depicts seem exceptional rather than part of a larger, national pattern.

Of course, understanding and effectively describing the bigger picture of hegemonic power relations in American society is tricky. It is always easier to see things in terms of good or bad individuals making simple choices. Those on the progressive left advocating for significant reform of the criminal justice system swam upstream for decades before concerns over mass incarceration became somewhat mainstream, even as reformist academics wrote reams of papers and books trying to connect the micro to the macro in legal processes.[50] Indeed, even in the political landscape of the 2020s when "defunding the police" is discussed openly, the term "structural problems" is in danger of becoming a catchphrase used rhetorically to bracket out what it itself refers to. It should not be surprising that entertainment programs produced or distributed by dominant media companies like Netflix and HBO have not lived up to the critical potential of the grassroots social movements interrogating hegemonic racism in the law, such as Black Lives Matter, that exploded in the 2010s–2020s.

But middlebrow crimesploitation like *How to Fix a Drug Scandal* claims a critical orientation. It addresses its viewers as smart, critical reasoners who are eager to delve beneath surface-level appearances. Ultimately, though, its fixation on individual culpability and mystery solving does little to subvert the status quo. When the focus of documentary inquiry is "Did he do it?" or "Who's to blame for this outrageous government failure?" systemic inequity, prejudice against outsiders, racism, sexism, and other forms of structural violence are bracketed. Indeed, a particularly distinguishing dimension of middlebrow crimesploitation is its whiteness. Cases that get the "deep dive" treatment that these middlebrow productions offer are rarely populated by Black or Latinx defendants, attorneys, or state actors. The whiteness of the protagonists and antagonists of these productions means that the question of how anti-Black racism shapes the administration of criminal justice in the United States is often ignored altogether.

Feigning Seriousness and Flattering the Viewer

Middlebrow crimesploitation, we have shown, presents itself as cerebral. Rather than manipulate viewers' emotions and cater to their lurid tastes, it seems to talk "up" to viewers, to treat them as critical thinkers. It sometimes does this by subtly distinguishing itself from its lowbrow counterparts. We saw, for instance, how *Making a Murderer* cast a jaundiced gaze upon the *Dateline* reporters eager to sensationalize Steven Avery's trial. One recent Netflix docuseries, *Don't F**k with Cats* (2019), directly tackled the question of its appeal to viewers' love for true crime programming.

Released in 2019 *Don't F**k with Cats* focuses on Internet sleuths chasing a person who posted online videos of himself first torturing and killing cats and later murdering a young man. The dramatic energy of the show comes from the dynamic between the sleuths and the killer, with significant airtime devoted to interviews with a woman named Deanna Thompson (who had adopted the internet name, "Baudi Moovan," an homage to the *Beastie Boys* tune "Body Movin'"), and a man named John Green. The show's title, as Thompson explains in the first moments of the series, refers to a norm (which Thompson calls "rule zero") that "you don't fuck with cats." The Internet, as Thompson tells us, is full of illicit but tolerated depictions of subjugation, destruction, and suffering. For some reason, though, harming cute animals such as housecats is deemed a bridge too far. Thompson, who self-identifies as a computer nerd, discovers via Facebook a video depicting a person placing two kittens into a plastic bag and sealing it with a vacuuming device, suffocating them. *Don't F**k with Cats* reconstructs the experience of viewing the video through an interaction with Thompson, alternating between what appear to be shots of her laptop screen (showing the video) and a headshot of her watching and narrating the video. Viewers of *Don't F**K with Cats* see live kittens being placed into a clear plastic bag by a human wearing a hood, but not the action of their killing. Instead, Thompson's reaction is the focus; she starts to cry and says, while the sound of the vacuuming device plays on her laptop, "It's fucking heartbreaking, dude. I hate this shit, dude."[51] It is a powerful introduction. The remainder of *Don't F**K with Cats* centers on Thompson's and Green's search for the hooded menace who killed the kittens.[52] Their vigilante investigation, mobilizing a whole cadre of Internet detectives through a Facebook group, culminates in their discovery of a video on a website, bestgore.com, depicting their cat killer murdering a young man. Prodding authorities, the vigilante detectives help international authorities to identify the killer as Luka Magnotta (née Eric Newman), a Canadian man. Magnotta is subsequently convicted for the murder of Jun Lin, a Chinese college student who had been living in Toronto.[53]

An implicit theme of *Don't F**k with Cats* is that the act of investigating—of satisfying the itch to unveil the truth—can have unintended consequences. The film suggests that its vigilante detectives' search for the mystery-person-who-fucked-with-cats—Luka Magnotta—ultimately drove Magnotta to move from animal torture to murder because he vainly thrived on the attention. Evoking old stereotypes of gay men as mentally ill and narcissistic, *Don't F**k with Cats* depicts Luka as a monster. We learn that he desperately craves attention. He has a history of impersonating others and setting up dozens of websites and social media accounts aimed at making himself into a celebrity. Viewers are led to believe that Luka lived in a sick fantasy world in which he was erotically playing out a gay version of Sharon Stone's psychopathic character in the 1992 movie *Basic Instinct*. His murder of Jun Lin was, the series suggests, a reenactment of the coital murder scene in the film. Surveillance footage, meanwhile, is plumbed to show us that while he was being questioned by authorities, he was performing *Basic Instinct*'s infamous "flashing" scene, in which Stone flashes her crotch during an interrogation scene by crossing and uncrossing her legs.[54]

For most of the series, the show encourages viewers to vicariously engage in the game of cat-and-mouse, where the cats are mousy Internet nerds working from home and the mouse is, we gradually learn, a glammed-up, globetrotting psychopath. There is no critique of the twenty-first-century attention economy, which rewards the commodification of the self into an Internet brand, turns likes and follows and reposts into a form of capital, and incentivizes the generation of controversial content. Aside from a few scathing remarks from Luka's mother, an obviously biased interview subject, there is no critique of Internet vigilantism. And there is no critique of the viewer's desire to vicariously roll up their sleeves alongside those internet vigilantes to figure out who is fucking with cats. The goal is to satisfy viewers' desires to safely venture into the darkest corners of the Internet and solve a mystery.

Until the final scene. At the very end of the serial Thompson changes roles. In a surprisingly reflective move, she moves from sleuth to critic. Noting that Magnotta seemed to feed on attention, she wonders whether her vigilante crusade may have fed into his pathology, pushing him to take his violent urges to the next level. "Did we feed the monster?" she wonders aloud. "Or did we create it?" Next, she breaks the fourth wall, turning her head to look directly toward the camera in order to address the viewer: "And you. You at home watching a whole fucking documentary on Luka Magnotta. Are you complicit?" The shot then changes to an animation of a curser logging out of Facebook while Thompson's voice says, "Perhaps it's time we turned off the machine."[55] Viewers of *Don't F**k with Cats* who watch until the finale end up not co-sleuths but co-conspirators.

Such meta-moments serve as a form of viewer flattery. *Don't F**k with Cats* seems to want to distinguish itself from other forms of crimesploitation. "You are more sophisticated than the folks who watch *Dateline* or *Cops*," such moments implicitly suggest to viewers. "You choose to spend your time watching quality television that challenges you to think about crime and punishment in new ways rather than offers you mindless thrills. You care about ethics and reason and the bigger picture." But asking viewers to think about the ethical consequences of consuming the docuseries they just watched is akin to telling consumers of a pork dish you have served them about the inhumane treatment of the pigs immediately after they have taken their last bite. The damage has been done. Any ethical awareness the series demonstrates seems undermined by the producers' decision to exhibit the docuseries. The coda substitutes a quick, unexpected confrontation with the viewers' voyeuristic desire for sustained analysis of the ideological origins and effects of crimesploitation that has been at the heart of this book. Inducing a fleeting sense of guilt in a viewer for her desire to gaze upon spectacles of cruelty, death, and online vigilantism, the show replicates the broader antistructuralism undergirding the rise of the punitive state: a conviction that individuals, rather than structures and forces that influence them, are the primary source of unethical behavior.

Taking Looking Seriously: Critical Visual Criminology and the Limits of Procedural Reform

While we have argued that the contemporary wave of true-crime documentaries often constitutes a middlebrow form of crimesploitation, we are not suggesting that all documentaries focused on individual cases are incapable of generating radical critiques of the criminal justice system. Stories about individuals *can* subvert dominant ideologies when they successfully connect the particular lives of persons to broader social structures.[56] But middlebrow crimesploitation usually fails to make those connections. It individualizes injustice by presenting it as the result of bad actors rather than an ordinary and predictable outcome of a society in which criminal punishment has become a primary method for addressing social problems.[57] It does not implicate viewers in the injustices it depicts; indeed, it turns cases involving immense pain and suffering into fodder for viewers to puzzle through a mystery or stick it to the man.

When middlebrow crimesploitation does gesture toward the structural context of the criminal justice system, it usually focuses on questions of protocols and procedures. Op-eds about *Making a Murderer* reveal, for instance, how the presentation of an individual case can generate a demand for a kind of systemic change that will do little to alleviate the vast majority of the injustice generated by the criminal justice system in an age of mass incarceration. Writing in the *Washington Post*, the director of the Wisconsin Innocence Project, Keith A. Findley, wrote,

> "Making a Murderer" is about more than Avery and Dassey's guilt or innocence, because the injustices the series suggest are hardly unique. The enduring takeaway ought to be the recognition that the criminal justice system, as a human system, is inevitably flawed. It does sometimes send innocent people to prison. And while most police, prosecutors, defense lawyers and judges are good, honest people who do their best to achieve justice, they do sometimes fail and even, on occasion, cross the line into misconduct in their zeal to secure what they perceive to be a just outcome.[58]

Procedural reforms, he went on to argue, are the solution: recording police interrogations, shielding forensic scientists from biasing information before they run tests on crime scene evidence, penalizing prosecutors who withhold exculpatory evidence from the defense. Such reforms will install, he argues, a humility that is so often lacking in the criminal justice system:

> The humility to recognize that sometimes we are wrong, even when we are most certain. The humility to recognize we are all affected by cognitive biases that can mislead us. The humility to recognize

that the system and the evidence it relies upon are flawed and can be improved. And the humility to recognize that when we occasionally get it wrong, we must do something about it.[59]

While humility is indeed a laudable quality to cultivate in those with the power to punish, Findley's argument—conditioned, perhaps, by the possibilities presented to viewers by *Making a Murderer*—is short-sighted. It does not consider how procedural reforms encode humility at a stage in the criminal justice system when much of the damage wrought by mass incarceration has already occurred. Standardized punishments for crime, the product of a 1970s effort to make time served for crimes more consistent, have already been set at harshly high levels.[60] Courts have shown extraordinarily high levels of tolerance for dangerous conditions in the prisons to which those found guilty are consigned.[61] Municipalities dependent on revenue from the policing of "broken windows" misdemeanors have created perverse incentives for police agencies to deprive poor people of their limited resources and, when they cannot pay, to take away their liberty. Much of the injustice plaguing criminal justice systems in the United States cannot be solved by procedural reform alone

Humility that *is* likely to prompt a reexamination of the foundations of the criminal justice system requires something more: a story that subverts the status quo by connecting an individual's particular experience of injustice to the problematic foundations of the criminal justice system rather than to the procedures and players that operate atop it. That might take the form of questioning the commonsense notion that "we cannot be safe without the police or the prison." Less radically, it might take the form of questioning the scope of legal violence (should it ever be used to respond to nonviolent crime?) or its severity (are death, life without parole, and solitary confinement forms of violence the state should be able to use against any person, regardless of what he or she has done?).[62] In the end, it is only by exposing the deep structure of law's violence and depicting that violence as cruel that "true life" stories of crime and punishment will actually invite critical responses.

Epilogue

W(h)ither Crimesploitation?

In 1993 a staffer on an early crimesploitation program, *American Detective*, engaged in an act of cultural whistleblowing. In an essay she wrote for *Harper's Magazine*, Debra Seagal wrote movingly of her work on the show as an indexer whose job it was to catalogue the hours of raw footage sent into the production offices by camera operators following police detectives around in cities across the country. What haunted her the most, she said, were the men and women on reams of unaired footage whose vulnerability was "too dark, too much like real life" to ever be aired. The dying AIDS patient busted for marijuana he was taking to alleviate his pain. The Vietnam veteran jailed for selling his prescription morphine to pay his rent. "I can peer into their private lives with the precision of a lab technician, replaying painful and sordid moments," she wrote.

> I am troubled that something of their humanity is stored indefinitely in our supervising producer's refrigerated video asylum. Some of their faces have even entered my dreamworld. This afternoon when I suggested that such unfortunates might be the real stars of our show, my boss snapped, "You empathize with the wrong people."[1]

The secret to reality television, Seagal suggested, was that it could not be too real. The criminals and their circumstances had to be just otherworldly enough to avoid triggering feelings of empathy from viewers.

That same year, James Wolcott wrote a review of *Cops* in the *New Yorker* that inadvertently captured that otherworldly quality. He told readers,

> My all-time favorite "Cops bust" . . . came when police were called
> to collar a huge naked black man during a robbery attempt. How
> he came to be naked no one knew. . . . Subduing him became an
> epic tussle, with four or five cops trying to cuff the wild man (his
> genitals obscured by an editing device) and everybody bouncing
> off the walls. When he was finally slammed to the floor, he stared
> straight at the camera and hollered, "Put my face in the papers!" It
> was as if an inmate had escaped from the collective unconscious—
> a taboo figure, the Naked Black Man with the Mad Grin. He
> tore a hole in reality, then returned, laughing, to the realm of the
> repressed, a reminder that race is still the joker card at the bottom
> of the deck. His arrest was practically a piece of performance art,
> the tragedy of slavery replayed as farce.[2]

Wolcott's tone was needlessly flippant, but his point about the show's
failure to adequately grapple with history illustrates Seagal's point about
crimesploitation's reluctance to get "too real." The nameless "Naked Black
Man with the Mad Grin" becomes a clown, a "joker," the carrier of a history that is not taken seriously. His over-the-top arrest paradoxically masks
the history of anti-Black violence it might have recalled. By turning suspects like this nameless man into modern-day minstrels, *Cops* kept the
explosive growth of the Black prison population in the late twentieth century—and the history of inequality that haunted it—from getting too real
for its white working- and middle-class viewers.

By keeping history and context at bay, crimesploitation shows like
Cops also earned the approval of authorities. As the executive producer of
Cops put it, police agencies generally welcomed *Cops* with open arms because
"we give equal time to the good guys for a change." When *Real Stories of
the Highway Patrol* premiered in 1993, the spokesperson for the California
Highway Patrol explained to a reporter from the *Sacramento Bee* that since
the roadside beating of Rodney King by Los Angeles police officers, "law
enforcement in general has been taking a bad rap."[3] With videos of officers
professionally managing (never harassing) a revolving cast of sideshow circus
acts (never victims of structural inequality), crimesploitation offered a way
for those who police the nation's poor to shore up their reputations.

Reality Meets "Reality"

In the past decade, however, it has become increasingly difficult to keep a lid on reality. With the rise of the Internet and the smartphone, millions of Americans gained the ability to record and publish video footage of police-civilian interactions that counter the neatly packaged offerings of crimesploitation shows. What was a long-shot in 1993—that a bystander to a roadside beating would have a video camera—had become, by 2020, a sure bet. That year the longest running crimesploitation show in history was taken down by a smartphone camera. On May 25 police responded to a 911 call from Cup Foods in Minneapolis. A store clerk reported that a man had tried to use a counterfeit bill. After identifying George Floyd as the man matching the clerk's description, the police handcuffed him and the parties struggled until Floyd ended up face down and handcuffed on the ground. Officer Derek Chauvin knelt on Floyd's neck while Floyd gasped for air and said he could not breathe. After about six minutes, Floyd became unresponsive while Chauvin kept his knee planted on Floyd's neck for another three silent minutes.[4]

Crucially, while Floyd was dying, seventeen-year-old Darnella Frazier pulled out her smartphone and began recording the scene. In this footage Chauvin looks down at Floyd's head while pinning his neck as Floyd begs to breathe and eventually becomes unconscious. In a grotesque gesture, Chauvin keeps his left hand on his hip in a way that seems nonchalant. Watching this, anyone might wonder: How can he kneel on his neck like that? How is it possible for that person to seem so uncaring and dismissive of human life? Why isn't anyone intervening? Can't this white cop see that he is killing this unarmed, handcuffed, prone Black man?

These moments crystalize the American criminal justice system in a way that is as vivid and unambiguous as anything since the Rodney King beating of thirty years ago. Everything about Chauvin's killing of George Floyd overflows with symbolism, connecting to spirals of meaning about race and law that have grown like fractals since the 1960s. The cops were called to respond to a minor crime involving a Black man; multiple officers came to the scene of this insignificant occurrence as though it were a major problem; officers handcuffed Floyd as soon as they were able to; the unarmed Floyd passively resisted officers but did not assault any of them; several non-Black officers forced Floyd's body face-down in the street; white officer Chauvin killed Floyd by pressing his bodyweight through his knee into Floyd's neck. The last part of the scene—the white cop's knee on the Black man's neck—said it all. A wave of protest exploded across the United States in the aftermath, adding fuel to the already blazing fire of unrest around racist police killings that had rekindled a few years before in Ferguson, Missouri.

The fallout was swift. Within days of Floyd's murder and the wave of protests across the nation, Paramount announced that it was canceling *Cops*. The A&E Network canceled *Live PD*, its lucrative, twenty-first-century version of *Cops*, which aired footage from police bodycams in real time. Headlines announcing the cancellation called *Cops* "Police Propaganda" and noted that critics had charged it with "Glorifying Police Aggression."[5]

The cancellations followed years of discontent about the show among community workers and organizers. For a long time local and national activist organizations had been organizing against *Cops*, with mixed success. In 2006 local activists organized a seventy-five-person protest at the city hall in Worcester, Massachusetts, to protest the city's decision to let *Cops* cameras to do ride-alongs with the Worcester Police Department. They successfully convinced the police chief to call off the agreement. "It exploits some people with some challenges," the chief acknowledged in a statement. "I just believe it is in the best interest to ask 'Cops' to leave."[6] But such wins were rare. On the national level, a campaign against the show was led by Color of Change, an online racial justice organization founded in 2005 by James Rucker and Van Jones to harness the power of Black Internet users. In 2013 the organization launched a campaign against *Cops*, accusing producers and corporate advertisers of building "a profit model around distorted and dehumanizing portrayals of Black Americans and the criminal justice system."[7]

What finally galvanized the movement against police violence and felled shows like *Cops*, though, was the popularization of the technical capacity to produce video and the rise of Internet platforms on which to disseminate it to a global audience. In the 1990s crimesploitation monopolized the market for video of police-civilian interactions. But now anyone can record and broadcast video of police-civilian interactions to a potential audience of millions. And they have. Since the 2000s public access to amateur recordings of police encounters with civilians has exploded. In fact, the eruptions of unrest that began in Ferguson, Missouri, in 2014 have largely been tied to smartphone footage of the police hurting and killing Black people. The most prominently known victims from the African American Policy Forum's "Say Their Names" movement were Black boys and men killed on camera by white police officers: Eric Garner, Tamir Rice, Walter Scott, Alton Sterling, Philando Castille, George Floyd. This rawer footage has starkly illustrated what activists have been saying for decades: that police violence against African Americans is often disproportionate and unjust. What is more, the verité style of "reality television," as we have noted, amplifies the way viewers respond to it; because they are understood to be "real," these videos are more likely to influence attitudes and beliefs than fiction.

The last decade, then, has witnessed noncorporate entities seizing that power of "the real" and offering a powerful counterdepiction of the world of law enforcement that crimesploitation has promulgated for decades. Americans are now watching the kind of video that producers of crimesploitation programs had long placed on ice—the "too dark, too much like real life" material that haunted *Harper's* essayist Debra Seagal's dreams. And many are disturbed by what they see.

Diminished Crimesploitation?

Given the events of 2020 it is tempting to argue that crimesploitation may be endangered by the realities of the criminal justice system that it has long papered over. Caution is warranted in making such claims, however. While we can tie the demise of *Cops* and *Live PD* to the effects of amateur video, it is important to remember that such videos are being released into a politically polarized public sphere in which a powerful, conservative countermobilization has arisen to parry challenges to police authority. The rise of the "Blue Lives Matter" movement—complete with its own modified version of the American flag—reveals how sacred the police are to many Americans. When amateur police violence videos begin circulating, *counter*-counternarratives quickly emerge to justify police behavior or smear the reputation of the victim—stymying the political potential of these videos to generate lasting change. There is, in short, a large demand among conservative Americans for the positive depictions of law enforcement that crimesploitation offers.

Rising fear of crime, meanwhile, provides the kinds of conditions in which crimesploitation's pro-authoritarian themes thrive. As of this writing, in the summer of 2021, "defund the police" continues to circulate as a wedge slogan as well as plausible-but-unlikely policy approach. But rising crime in the nation's cities seems to have dampened state actors' willingness to radically rethink policing. In San Diego, where one of us lives, the mayor just proposed a significant increase in funding for the city police department.[8] In Atlanta, where the other lives, crime became the central issue in the 2021 mayoral campaign, with multiple candidates in the Democratic stronghold proposing an expansion of the police on the city's streets.[9] Indeed, legislative action and political change was sluggish in the aftermath of the national wave of protests in response to the killing of George Floyd. Even with the 2021 inauguration of Joe Biden and Democratic majorities in the House and Senate, a federal police reform bill bearing George Floyd's name was not enacted in time for the one-year anniversary of George Floyd's death, a deadline for which President Biden had strongly advocated.[10] As fear of crime rises in the nation, skepticism of the police began to wane: after a five-point dip to 48 percent in 2020—its lowest in decades—support for the police rose in 2021 to 51 percent, the only institution in Gallup's survey of Americans trust in private and public institutions in which confidence grew.[11] The cancellation of *Cops* and *Live PD* may ultimately turn out to have been a flash in the pan.

Drugs and Podcasts: New Trends in Crimesploitation

While policing shows appear to be temporarily on the skids, they are only a subset of crimesploitation programming. Despite the cancellation of *Cops*, there are numerous choices for casual viewers looking for "real" cops, robbers, and true crime mysteries.[12] These and other crimesploitation programs focused on addiction, criminal activity, government scandals, murder cases, and punishment continue to exploit their subjects and normalize the neoliberal carceral state. Some parts of the crimesploitation universe are even expanding. Recently, *Drugs, Inc.*, *Intervention*, and other shows featuring drug use and dealing have become prominent fixtures in the streaming universe. In its current collection of original documentaries, Netflix has a large handful of serial investigative programs exploring drug trafficking with an abundance of screen time devoted to masked dealers displaying guns and piles of drugs while bragging about their product.[13] And while these "reality narco" shows give viewers an up-close view of border patrol agents working drug interdiction and dealers sporting bandanas, balaclavas, and chromed guns, the true protagonists often seem to be the drugs themselves, frequently in enormous quantities. Unlike the reality of personal drug intoxication for actual users in America, which entails sniffing, smoking, or injecting a few tiny grains of heroin, cocaine, or meth, narco-TV shows off baseball-sized lumps of heroin, fist-sized shards of crystal, and piles of cocaine spilled over countertops. In the same sense that "food porn" is used to describe luscious images of fancy meals on cooking shows like *Top Chef*, "drug porn" seems an apt description of the drug imagery on these narco-shows. These fetishistic shots of forbidden substances set the stage for scenes that dramatize drug mules crossing the US border in vehicles packed with drugs. Viewers get sutured into the passenger seat, "riding shotgun" while the driver narrates his or her strategies and thrills when crossing the border. In one episode, a mule throws his hands in the air after crossing, cheers, and says he feels "like a bandit!"[14]

But perhaps the most significant development in the recent cultural history of crimesploitation has been the rise of true crime podcasts, a profitable and growing media form.[15] Crime programs have consistently led the podcast genre, most prominently with *Serial*'s blockbuster success in 2014. Notable examples include *Casefile* (an Australia-based cold case investigation show), *Serial Killers* (psychological profiles of serial killers in a storytelling format), *Black Girl Missing* (highlighting the oft-neglected cases of Black girl victims in the United States), *The Generation Why* (two friends discuss mysterious crimes), as well as programs with a more black comedy flavor such as *My Favorite Murder* (snarky comedians juggle casefile retellings with improv humor and feminist discourses) and *Last Podcast on the Left* (a raunchy "bro" alternative to *My Favorite Murder*).[16] Crime podcasts represent one of the pillars of this profitable and growing media form.

These true crime podcasts vary in their focus and ideological orientation. Some are simply crimesploitation in a new medium. The title of a program like *My Favorite Murder* says it all. It is a flagrantly undisguised effort to commodify murder, obscuring the humanity of all those whose lives are permanently ended or traumatized by homicide. Other programs like the first season of *Serial* take on a more middlebrow veneer, satisfying viewers' desire to play detective by offering them the chance to reopen, along with intrepid journalists, a murder case to see if a defendant was properly convicted (or acquitted). And yet other programs have effectively served as counterpoints to crimesploitation, pushing viewers to recognize the relationship between individual cases and structural patterns and problems with the administration of justice in the United States. *Vulture*'s 2019 top-10 list of podcasts included a meta-crimesploitation podcast called *Headlong: Running from Cops*, which explored the phenomenon of *Cops* in American culture, unveiling the show's exploitative dimensions.[17] Season 1 of American

Public Media's *In the Dark* revisited the case of Jacob Wetterling, an eleven-year-old boy who was abducted and killed in Minnesota in 1989.[18] Journalist Madeleine Baran placed the heavily sensationalized case, which fed into the "stranger danger" panic of the 1980s and 1990s, into a broader context. Among other things, the show punctured the myth that stranger abduction of children was common, profiled the negative effects that political pressure to find Wetterling's killer had on the police work done in the case (and the effect the rush-to-judgment had on innocent men in the community), and called into question the efficacy and value of sex offender registries that were the legacy of this sort of case. Ideologically, crime stories seem more "up for grabs" in the podcast universe than in the television universe.

From Sympathy to Empathy

Battered but not broken, crimesploitation continues to legitimize a neoliberal carceral state that values order more than justice and human docility more than human flourishing. It continues to offer viewers the chance to escape from and vicariously resist, as well as recommit to, bearing the burdens of life when the state has largely abandoned its commitments to the common good. By treating crimesploitation as a symptom of a particular historical moment, we have attempted to denaturalize it, to disrupt the "common sense" ideas about crime, authority, and governance that it peddles.

And by emphasizing its commodification of others' pain, we have attempted to call attention to how exploitative and immoral it is. We began this book by noting that crimesploitation is distinct from the classical and modern exploitation films that preceded it. In those earlier media, that which was exploited was the taboo. Its critics, of course, saw the consumption of these media as reinforcing pernicious stereotypes in the popular imagination, from the depiction of tribal peoples as cannibals in classical exploitation films to the NAACP's objection to the depiction of Black men as hypersexual in Blacksploitation films. But those who appeared on screen were always actors playing parts. In contrast, those who appear in crimesploitation are often vulnerable persons who, after signing releases, are exploited for the pleasure of millions. Their shame or shamelessness is commodified and packaged into a product that is sold to advertisers and audiences. The pleasures these programs offer, we have shown, are derived from others' pain and degradation. It is a particularly pernicious "regime of representation."[19]

But when crimesploitation succeeds, it is not only by exploiting the misfortunes of the "failed citizens" it depicts, but also by exploiting the fears and desires and prejudices of the viewers it entertains. For the millions of Americans who watch crimesploitation programs, a true reckoning with its exploitative nature is unlikely to happen until they see themselves as exploited, until they see the "othered" on television sets not as pitiful individuals but as fellow subjects of a broader regime of representation that exploits performer and spectator alike. In the end, crimesploitation's fate may not depend on sympathy *for* the exploited but on empathy *with* them.

Notes

Introduction: The Disciplined and the Delinquent

1. Kevin D. Thompson, "Arresting Television," Cox News Service, February 8, 2002; L. Hetherington, "Raw Reality Makes Successful Shows," *Herald Sun* (Melbourne, Australia), October 23, 1991.

2. June Deery offers an overview of the struggle to define the term, settling on "staged actuality," which captures reality television as "a non-fictional presentation of actual events occurring in the empirical world as experienced by amateur participants who have not been hired to act as someone other than themselves or to write a program-length script" yet acknowledges the role that producers play in planning and structuring these events. June Deery, *Reality TV* (Cambridge: Polity Press, 2015), 29, 31. There is a voluminous literature on reality television. Our approach to it is largely informed by scholarly work that has linked it to the rise of neoliberalism in the late twentieth century, especially James Hay and Laurie Ouellette, *Better Living Through TV: Television and Post-Welfare Citizenship* (Oxford: Blackwell, 2008).

3. The sheer number of crimesploitation shows that have emerged since *Cops* premiered in 1988 demonstrate its success. In 2011 Laurie Ouellette catalogued a large list to which we have added others, yet this list is likely still incomplete: *Real Stories of the Highway Patrol* (1993–98), *LAPD: Life on the Beat* (1995–99), *American Detective* (1991–93), *Rookies* (2008–9), *Top Cops* (1990–93), *Lockup* (2005–17), *Lockdown* (2007), *The Wanted* (2009), *Video Justice* (2006–7), *Manhunters* (2009–11), *Breaking Down the Bars* (2011), *Hard Time* (2011–13), *Breakout* (2010–13), *Homeland Security USA* (2009), *Police Women of Broward County* (2009–11), *Bounty Girls: Miami* (2007), *Southern Fried Stings* (2010–11), *Undercover Stings* (2012), *Jacked: Auto Theft Task Force* (2008), *Speeders* (2007–9), *Parking Wars* (2008–12), *DEA* (2008–9), *Bait Car* (2007–12), *Mall Cops* (2010), *Alaska State Troopers* (2009–15), *Operation Repo* (2007–14), *Jail* (2007–10), *Cajun Justice* (2012), *Jail: Las Vegas* (2015–), *I (Almost) Got Away with It* (2010–16), *Inside American Jail* (2007–9), *No Excuses with Master P* (2009), *T.I.'s Road to Redemption* (2009), *Smile . . . You're Under Arrest!* (2008–9), *Steven Seagal:*

Lawman (2009–14), *Intervention* (2005–), *Gangland* (2007–10), *Louisiana Lockdown* (2012), and *Dog the Bounty Hunter* (2004–12). Laurie Ouellette, "Real Justice: Law and Order on Reality Television," in *Imagining Legality: Where Law Meets Popular Culture*, ed. Austin Sarat (Tuscaloosa: University of Alabama Press, 2011), 152–76.

4. Harry F. Waters, "TV's Crime Wave Gets Real," *Newsweek*, May 15, 1989, 72.

5. Mark Washburn, "Successful Cops Cuffs Its 500th Show," *Pittsburgh Post-Gazette*, April 27, 2002.

6. The best-known exploitation films are the "Blaxploitation" films of the 1970s, including Ossie Davis's *Cotton Comes to Harlem* (1970), Gordon Parks's *Shaft* (1971), and Melvin Van Peebles's *Sweet Sweetback's Baadasssss Song* (1971). True crime texts, as we have argued, span the gamut from highbrow to lowbrow. Among the highbrow fare, the best known are Truman Capote's *In Cold Blood* (1966) and Norman Mailer's *The Executioner's Song* (1979). Few lowbrow true crime texts have stood the test of time, but examples might include works by Ann Rule, especially *The Stranger Beside Me: The Shocking Inside Story of Serial Killer Ted Bundy*, which began as a memoir in 1980 and was reprinted with updates periodically until 2008.

7. Michel Foucault, *Discipline and Punish: The Birth of the Prison* (Paris: Editions Gallimard, 1975); English translation by Alan Sheridan (New York: Vintage Books, 1995), 286. Citations refer to the Vintage edition.

8. Joy Wiltenburg, "True Crime: The Origins of Modern Sensationalism," *American Historical Review* 109, no. 5 (2004): 1377–1404.

9. *A Narrative of the Captivity and Restoration of Mrs. Mary Rowlandson* (1682). The text was published under various titles in subsequent centuries.

10. Kristin Boudreau, *The Spectacle of Death: Populist Literary Responses to American Capital Cases* (Amherst, NY: Prometheus Books, 2006).

11. See, e.g., Martha Merrill Umphrey, "Media Melodrama! Sensationalism and the 1907 Trial of Harry Thaw," *New York Law School Law Review* 43 (1999): 715–40.

12. Gray Cavender and Mark Fishman, "Television Reality Crime Programs: Context and History," in *Entertaining Crime: Television Reality Programs*, ed. Fishman and Cavender (New York: Walter de Gruyter, 1998), 3–15, 8.

13. FBI agents never killed anyone in the show's latter seasons. "Banned, too, was behavior that was familiar to many people who had been interviewed by agents from the Bureau. On television, FBI personnel were always polite to citizens, solicitous of their feelings, and 'very kind.' They never lied on the witness stand." While the skittish, image-obsessed Hoover would occasionally get cold feet about the show, he was pleased enough with it that he told one graduating class of the FBI's academy to treat the star of the show, a stand-in for himself, as a role model. Curt Gentry, *J. Edgar Hoover: The Man and the Secrets* (New York: W. W. Norton, 1991), 582. Hoover's cooperation with the program, which attracted 40 million viewers weekly, paid him handsomely. He reportedly earned $75,000–$100,000 per episode. David Friedman, "Wanted: Lowlifes and High Ratings," *Rolling Stone*, January 12, 1989. A similar dynamic existed between the LAPD's revolutionary mid-century chief of police William H. (Bill) Parker and the trailblazing program *Dragnet*. See Joe Dominick, *Blue: The LAPD and the Battle to Redeem American Policing* (New York: Simon and Schuster, 2015), 28.

14. Cavender and Fishman, "Television Reality Crime Programs," 10. Cavender and Fishman note that *True Detective Mysteries*, one of the many true crime radio shows of the 1930s, had pioneered this call for community involvement in crime fighting.

15. Eric Schaefer, *Bold! Daring! Shocking! True! A History of Exploitation Films, 1919–1959* (Durham, NC: Duke University Press, 1999), 3, 267, 69, 220.

16. Calum Waddell, *The Style of Sleaze: The American Exploitation Film, 1959–1977* (Edinburgh: Edinburgh University Press, 2018), 8, 141. While they were condemned by the NAACP, Blaxploitation films were produced by Black artists and aimed at Black audiences. Many have read them as counterhegemonic. Their sensational content existed "alongside an aspirational presentation of grassroots rebellion. It is this urban opposition to (typically) government or police authority that exploits any anti-establishment rhetoric" (143). One critic has argued that some Blaxploitation films were critical responses to the era's reactionary police vigilante films like *Dirty Harry*. Sweetback, the titular character of *Sweet Sweetback's Baadasss Song*, was the opposite of the white vigilante cop, "a fact emphasized by each film's opening dedication: *Sweetback*'s 'to all those brothers and sisters who had enough of The Man,' and *Dirty Harry*'s 'to the police officers of San Francisco who gave their lives in the line of duty.'" Paula J. Massood, *Black City Cinema: African American Urban Experiences in Film* (Philadelphia: Temple University Press, 2003), 96.

17. One now finds a whole range of lesser-known 'sploitations in the vocabulary of cultural critics and connoisseurs, from "Canuxploitation" (Canadian B-movies) to "Nunsploitation" (nuns behaving badly).

18. Waddell, *The Style of Sleaze*, 186.

19. Massood, *Black City Cinema*, 103.

20. Cavender and Fishman, "Television Reality Crime Programs."

21. Deery, *Reality TV*.

22. Cavender and Fishman, "Television Reality Crime Programs."

23. Nixon-Agnew Victory Committee, "The First Civil Right" (1968 campaign ad), "The Living Room Candidate: Presidential Campaign Commercials, 1952–2020," Museum of the Moving Image (New York), http://www.livingroomcandidate.org/commercials/1968/the-first-civil-right (accessed July 6, 2021). Naomi Murakawa has noted that the "first civil right" was initially used by members of Harry Truman's administration to refer to the right of African Americans to be protected from white supremacist violence. See Murakawa, *The First Civil Right: How Liberals Built Prison America* (New York: Oxford University Press, 2014).

24. Jenifer Warren, "One in 100: Behind Bars in America 2008," Pew Charitable Trusts, February 28, 2008, http://www.pewtrusts.org/en/research-and-analysis/reports/2008/02/28/one-in-100-behind-bars-in-america-2008 (accessed August 31, 2020).

25. Godfrey Hodgson, *America in Our Time: From World War II to Nixon—What Happened and Why* (Princeton, NJ: Princeton University Press, 1976).

26. David Harvey, *A Brief History of Neoliberalism* (Oxford: Oxford University Press, 2007).

27. From 1980 to 2017, inflation-adjusted median hourly wages for workers with high school or less than high school education never exceeded what they were in 1979. They bottomed out in 1996, when workers with a high school education but no college were making

11% less than what they would have made in 1979, and workers with less than a high school education were making 25% less than what they would have made in 1979. In 1988, these workers were making 5.1% and 14.3% less than they would have made in 1979. John Schmitt, Elise Gould, and Josh Bivens, "America's Slow-Motion Wage Crisis: Four Decades of Slow and Unequal Growth," Economic Policy Institute, September 13, 2018, https://files.epi.org/pdf/153535.pdf (accessed August 31, 2020).

28. This theory of capitalism, known as "racial capitalism," rejects the conventional Marxian notion, espoused by scholars like Adolph Reed Jr., that racism is one of a number of "ideologies of ascriptive hierarchy that stabilize capitalist social reproduction." Adolph Reed Jr., "Marx, Race, and Neoliberalism," *New Labor Forum* 22, no. 1 (2013): 49–57, 53. Instead, it argues that from its inception the "development, organization, and expansion of capitalist society pursued *essentially* racial directions." Indeed, capitalism developed in tandem with, rather than in spite of, the unwaged labor of slavery. Cedric J. Robinson, *Black Marxism: The Making of the Black Radical Tradition* (Chapel Hill: University of North Carolina Press, 1983), 2 (emphasis added). As Siddhant Isaar glosses it, the theory of racial capitalism explains "the persistence of racial domination within capitalist society without treating race as merely superstructural or irrelevant to regimes of capital accumulation." Neoliberalism represents continuity with two major elements in the history of capitalism: "First, racialized non-white populations, always bounded within a historically specific context, undergird regimes of normative wage-labor and face forms of expropriation that exceed capitalist exploitation. And, second, the reproduction of the system of racial capitalism is only possible because of a cross-class alliance between political and economic elites and a portion of the working class brought together by white supremacy." Isaar, "Listening to Black Lives Matter: Racial Capitalism and the Critique of Neoliberalism," *Contemporary Political Theory* 20 (2021): 48–71, 57, 63.

29. On the purposeful discrimination written into mid-twentieth-century welfare programs and labor laws, see Ira Katznelson, *When Affirmative Action Was White: An Untold History of Racial Inequality in Twentieth-Century America* (New York: W. W. Norton, 2005).

30. On the prison as a form of "surplus" management of the poor, see Ruth Wilson Gilmore, *Golden Gulag: Prisons, Surplus, Crisis, and Opposition in Globalizing California* (Berkeley: University of California Press, 2007).

31. Carl Suddler, *Presumed Criminal: Black Youth and the Justice System in Postwar New York* (New York: NYU Press, 2019). On the role that discourses of pathology played in the development of the late twentieth-century carceral state, see Murakawa, *The First Civil Right*, and Elizabeth Hinton, *From the War on Poverty to the War on Crime: The Making of Mass Incarceration in America* (Cambridge, MA: Harvard University Press, 2016). Crime in these communities was often the result of dwindling economic opportunity and the hopelessness that came with it: a turn to work in illegal economic activities, the violence that results from the lack of legal ways to resolve disputes in illegal markets, drug abuse, and the crimes that sometimes become necessary to support an addiction.

32. On the racial consequences of the war on drugs, see Michael Tonry, *Malign Neglect: Race, Crime, and Punishment in America* (New York: Oxford University Press, 1995). On

mass incarceration as a modern iteration of Jim Crow, see Michelle Alexander, *The New Jim Crow: Mass Incarceration in the Age of Colorblindness* (New York: The New Press, 2010).

33. Stephen Dillon, *Fugitive Life: The Queer Politics of the Prison State* (Durham, NC: Duke University Press, 2018), 9.

34. Elayne Rapping, "Aliens, Nomads, Mad Dogs, and Road Warriors: The Changing Face of Criminal Violence on TV," in *Reality TV: Remaking Television Culture*, ed. Susan Murray and Laurie Ouellette (New York: NYU Press, 2004), 214–30, 221. Rapping overlooks the extent to which fictional crime films in the late twentieth century could themselves portray criminals as psychopaths driven by irrational instincts to do evil. Blockbuster vigilante films of the 1970s, for instance, portrayed street criminals as parasitical marauders motivated more by the desire to sow chaos than to advance their own self-interest (*Death Wish*) or to satisfy deviant brute, sadistic instincts (*Dirty Harry*).

35. Nicole Rafter and Michelle Brown have called the generation of criminological folk knowledge "popular criminology." See Nicole Rafter and Michelle Brown, *Criminology Goes to the Movies: Crime Theory and Popular Culture* (New York: NYU Press, 2011).

36. These programs address a "we" that they imagine as ordinary, law-abiding, middle-class Americans. When we use "we" in the context of discussing the ideology of these shows, we are referring to this imagined "we."

37. The state's withdrawal of its prior claim to be able to prevent crime is a key feature of what David Garland calls the "culture of control." Garland, *The Culture of Control: Crime and Social Order in Contemporary Society* (Chicago: University of Chicago Press, 2001).

38. Michelle Brown, *The Culture of Punishment: Prison, Society, and Spectacle* (New York: New York University Press, 2009), 13.

39. The scholarly literature documenting the outsized effect of reality television on viewers includes James W. Potter, "Perceived Reality in Television Effects Research," *Journal of Broadcasting and Electronic Media* 39, no. 1 (1995): 496–516; Judith Van Evra, *Television and Child Development* (Hillsdale, NJ: Lawrence Erlbaum, 1990); Ron Tamborini, Dolf Zillmann, and J. Jennings Bryant, "Fear and Victimization: Exposure to Television and Perceptions of Crime and Fear," *Annals of the International Communication Association* 8, no. 1 (1984): 492–513. Summarizing this literature, Mary Beth Oliver and G. Blake Armstrong write, "Media content that is perceived by the viewer as real or realistic is thought to have stronger effects on attitudes, beliefs, and behaviors than is media content that is understood to be fictional." Mary Beth Oliver and G. Blake Armstrong, "The Color of Crime: Perceptions of Caucasians' and African-Americans' Involvement in Crime," in *Entertaining Crime*, ed. Fishman and Cavender, 19–36, 24. In their own research, Oliver and Armstrong found that exposure to reality-based TV was a significant predictor of people's perception that there is a high prevalence of crime, while fictional television was not a significant predictor of their perception of crime prevalence or was only marginally associated with it.

40. For instance, many viewers identified with the bigoted Archie Bunker on the television show *All in the Family* (1971–79), even though the show was satirizing the character. Neil Vidmar and Milton Rokeach, "Archie Bunker's Bigotry: A Study in Selective Perception and Exposure," *Journal of Communication* 24, no. 1 (1974): 36–47.

41. Lawrence W. Levine, "The Folklore of Industrial Society: Popular Culture and Its Audiences," *American Historical Review* 97, no. 5 (1992): 1369–99.

42. Janice A. Radway, *Reading the Romance: Women, Patriarchy, and Popular Literature* (Chapel Hill: University of North Carolina Press, 1984).

43. "'Yes, I like a happy ending,' a twelve-year-old boy told an interviewer [in 1949], 'but once in a while I'd like to see the criminal get away.'" Levine, "The Folklore of Industrial Society," 1379.

44. Foucault, *Discipline and Punish*. For a helpful overview of modernity and the cultural response to it, see Ben Singer, *Melodrama and Modernity: Early Sensational Cinema and Its Contexts* (New York: Columbia University Press, 2001), especially chap. 1, "Meanings of Modernity."

45. Debra Seagal, "Tales from the Cutting Room Floor: The Reality of 'Reality-Based' Television," *Harper's Magazine*, November 1993, 51.

46. In this sort of fetishization of death and disorder, crimesploitation was not unique among popular culture. Indeed, along with comic books, crime fiction, and television shows, it brought to the small screen what a long line of fictional crime films, from *The Public Enemy* (1931) to *Bonnie and Clyde* (1967) to *No Country for Old Men* (2007) had long offered Americans: "a cultural space for the expression of resistance to authority" or "the pleasure of rebellion within safe constraints." Like crimesploitation, many of these crime films seduced viewers with the pleasures of rebellion and chaos while ultimately offering endings that upheld a conservative commitment to social order and control. But for those who "like to see the criminal get away" the ending may not matter; vicariously identifying with the bad boys before they get caught may be its own kind of reward. Nicole Rafter, *Shots in the Mirror: Crime Films and Society* (Oxford: Oxford University Press, 2006), 13, 17.

47. Elisabeth R. Anker, *Orgies of Feeling: Melodrama and the Politics of Freedom* (Durham, NC: Duke University Press, 2014), 111.

48. James Parker, "Prison Porn," *The Atlantic*, March 2010, 36–37, 37.

49. Schaefer, *Bold! Daring! Shocking! True!* 341–42.

1. Humilitainment, Inc.

1. There is a voluminous literature on the "punitive turn" in late twentieth-century American history, the decline of welfarist approaches to punishment and the ratcheting up of harsh punishment in its stead. Accounts we rely upon include David Garland, *The Culture of Control: Crime and Social Order in Contemporary Society* (Chicago: University of Chicago Press, 2001); Elizabeth Hinton, *From the War on Poverty to the War on Crime: The Making of Mass Incarceration in America* (Cambridge: Harvard University Press, 2016); Elaine Tyler May, *Fortress America: How We Embraced Fear and Abandoned Democracy* (New York: Basic Books, 2017); James Forman Jr., *Locking Up Our Own: Crime and Punishment in Black America* (New York: Farrar, Straus, and Giroux, 2017); and Naomi Murakawa, *The First Civil Right: How Liberals Built Prison America* (New York: Oxford University Press, 2014).

2. On child abduction panic in the 1980s, see Paul M. Renfro, *Stranger Danger: Family Values, Childhood, and the American Carceral State* (New York: Oxford University Press, 2020).

3. The ADT Corporation, Home Security Commercial, 1992, video, https://www.youtube.com/watch?v=CIwPNWwpDZo.

4. In our current era of criminal justice reform, it can be easy to look back upon this fear as irrational. And it often was. The panics about child kidnapping and sexual abuse and the rapes of women in dark alleyways and parks were profoundly misplaced. Women and children were much more likely to be harmed in their own homes and neighborhoods than in public spaces. And their assailants were more likely to be family members and acquaintances, rather than strangers. May, *Fortress America*. Perhaps more important, the fixation on the victimization of (white) middle-class people vastly overstated the likelihood of their victimization—and ignored just how disproportionately victimized by violent crime people of color and the poor were. When murder rates were reaching their highs in the 1980s, Lisa L. Miller has noted, the lifetime risk of being murdered was 1 in 238 for white Americans and 1 in 34 for Black Americans, many of whom were concentrated in impoverished cities as a result of systematic exclusion from the nation's suburbs. Had the homicide rates at their peak persisted indefinitely, an African American man would have had a 1 in 17 risk over the course of his life of becoming the victim of homicide. Lisa L. Miller, *The Myth of Mob Rule: Violent Crime and Democratic Politics* (New York: Oxford University Press, 2016).

5. Ann L. Pastore and Kathleen Maguire, eds., *Sourcebook of Criminal Justice Statistics 2003* (Albany, NY: The Hindelang Criminal Justice Research Center, 2005), 106.

6. Legitimacy had become a concern for state actors, who faced political blowback over rising crime rates. Politicians responded, as we have seen, by ratcheting up the consequences for crime. But they also sought to lower their constituents' expectations about what the state could do. The state would punish those criminals it caught severely, they promised, but the police could not be everywhere. Everyone, from corporations to homeowners to pedestrians out for an evening stroll, had the responsibility to surveil their personal surroundings and ensure that they did not give rise to opportunities for crime. From encouraging participation in neighborhood watch groups to offering the public access to sex offender registries, the state hammered home a tacit message: private actors were the partners in, rather than the mere beneficiaries of, the work undertaken by law enforcement agencies. Beyond punishment, the state's role in criminal justice matters was no longer to "command and control but rather to persuade and align, to organize, to ensure that other actors play their part." Garland, *The Culture of Control*, 126. Elaine Tyler May fascinatingly traces the rise of this "do it yourself" approach to public safety to Cold War era disaster planning. See *Fortress America*.

7. Jonathan Markovitz, *Legacies of Lynching: Racial Violence and Memory* (Minneapolis: University of Minnesota Press, 2004).

8. Grace Elizabeth Hale, *Making Whiteness: The Culture of Segregation in the South, 1890–1940* (New York: Pantheon Books, 1998), 237.

9. Life sometimes imitated art, however, as in the case of Bernhard Goetz, a New York man who shot and wounded four Black teenagers on a New York City subway in 1984 after they surrounded him and demanded five dollars. Goetz became, in some quarters, a populist hero—the "subway vigilante" who fought back against an increasingly lawless society. In subsequent decades, the liberalization of the law of self-defense in "stand your ground" laws

led to several acts of vigilante killing, most notoriously neighborhood watchman George Zimmerman's killing of Trayvon Martin, a Black teenager whom he shot in an altercation as Martin walked home from a nearby store.

10. Take, for instance, George H. W. Bush's campaign for president in 1988. Along with an infamous race-baiting ad that boasted of his support for the death penalty, Bush explained to voters that his approach to criminal justice policy was best summed up by a line from *Dirty Harry: Sudden Impact* (1983): "Go ahead: Make my day." Qtd. in Daniel LaChance, *Executing Freedom: The Cultural Life of Capital Punishment in the United States* (Chicago: University of Chicago Press, 2016), 50.

11. Lary May, "Redeeming the Lost War: Backlash Films and the Rise of the Punitive State," in *Punishment in Popular Culture*, ed. Charles J. Ogletree Jr. and Austin Sarat (New York: NYU Press, 2015), 23–54.

12. Ian Haney Lopez, *Dog Whistle Politics: How Coded Racial Appeals Have Reinvented Racism and Wrecked the Middle Class* (New York: Oxford University Press, 2014).

13. On whiteness and "white trash," see Matt Wray, *Not Quite White: White Trash and the Boundaries of Whiteness* (Durham, NC: Duke University Press, 2006).

14. Kevin Glynn, *Tabloid Culture: Trash Taste, Popular Power, and the Transformation of American Television* (Durham, NC: Duke University Press, 2000), 37.

15. Qtd. in Pamela Donovan, "Armed with the Power of Television: Reality Crime Programming and the Reconstruction of Law and Order in the United States," in *Entertaining Crime: Television Reality Programs*, ed. Mark Fishman and Gray Cavender (New York: Walter de Gruyter, 1998), 125.

16. Qtd. in ibid., 124.

17. Glynn, *Tabloid Culture*, 37.

18. Qtd. in ibid.

19. Austin Sarat, Madeline Chan, Maia Cole, et al., "Scenes of Execution: Spectatorship, Political Responsibility, and State Killing in American Film," in *Punishment in Popular Culture*, ed. Ogletree and Sarat, 199–235.

20. Shortly after the program grew into a national phenomenon, Von Erck was critically examined in the media. The *New York Daily News* called him a "community college dropout," noted that he had changed his name from Phillip John Eide to something more "exotic," and quoted portions of Von Erck's blog, http://www.angrygerman.com, that were bizarrely critical of a kidnapping victim in the Iraq war who had participated in his captors' propaganda videos ("Let me be the first and probably only American to wish for his speedy death," the *Daily News* reported him as writing). Lloyd Grove, "Predator Comes with a Big Catch," *New York Daily News*, September 7, 2006. A profile of Perverted Justice in the *New York Times* presented Von Erck as an obsessed, tortured soul who grew up the child of an alcoholic: "In many ways, Mr. Von Erck, who said he and his mother moved 13 times when he was in high school because they were often short of money, continues to live that messy life of deprivation. His meals often consist of ramen noodles, he said; his bed is perpetually unmade. For years, he has been trying unsuccessfully to find his father, who, he says, still owes his mother child support. 'I have a low opinion of men in general,' he said." Show-

ing an Oedipal undercurrent to Von Erck's crusade and noting how obsessive he is about ferreting out potential sex offenders ("Every waking minute he's on that computer," Von Erck's mother told the newspaper's reporter), the *New York Times* identified irrational and personal elements of Von Erck's vigilantism. Allen Salkin, "Website Hunts Pedophiles, and TV Goes Along," *New York Times*, December 13, 2006.

21. Salkin, "Website Hunts Pedophiles, and TV Goes Along."

22. Renfro, *Stranger Danger*.

23. Robert O. Self, *All in the Family: The Realignment of American Democracy Since the 1960s* (New York: Hill and Wang, 2012).

24. On sex panics and neoliberal values, see Roger N. Lancaster, *Sex Panic and the Punitive State* (Berkeley: University of California Press, 2011), and Renfro, *Stranger Danger*. On the broader history of constructions of the sex offender, see Philip Jenkins, *Moral Panic: Changing Concepts of the Child Molester in Modern America* (New Haven, CT: Yale University Press, 1998), and Chrysanthi S. Leon, *Sex Fiends, Perverts, and Pedophiles: Understanding Sex Crime Policy in America* (New York: NYU Press, 2011).

25. To be sure, we are not suggesting that adults who seek out sex with adolescents are the carriers of some emancipatory queer sensibility that is being oppressed here. While *To Catch a Predator* conflates sexual desire for adolescents with sexual desire for young children; paternalistically treats adolescents as lacking judgment; and fails to distinguish between "predators" in their early twenties and those in their forties, there is a power asymmetry between adults and adolescents that makes the exploitation and coercion of teenagers by adults a reason to ban the behavior. We suggest, rather, that the pedophile inspires fear and loathing *not solely* in response to the potential harm he causes to minors, but also in response to the more abstract threat he embodies: the destruction of the family.

26. "Flagler Beach, Florida: Part 1," episode 16 of *Dateline NBC: To Catch a Predator*, hosted by Chris Hansen, aired February 27, 2007, on MSNBC.

27. In its celebration of the act of surveillance, *To Catch a Predator* follows a tradition in reality television of acculturating viewers to a world that is increasingly surveilled and reconciling such surveillance with populist and democratic values. As Mark Andrejevic has argued, though, corporations and the state are the primary beneficiaries of a surveillance culture. See *Reality TV: The Work of Being Watched* (Lanham, MD: Rowman and Littlefield, 2004).

28. "Fairfax County, Virginia," episode 2 of *Dateline NBC: To Catch a Predator*, executive produced by Donna G. Johnson, aired November 4, 2005, on MSNBC.

29. "Riverside County, California," episode 3 of *Dateline NBC: To Catch a Predator*, executive produced by Donna G. Johnson, aired February 3, 2006, on MSNBC.

30. Jack Katz, *Seductions of Crime: Moral and Sensual Attractions in Doing Evil* (New York: Basic Books, 1988), 27.

31. Amy Adler, "To Catch a Predator," *Columbia Journal of Gender and Law* 21 (2011): 530–60.

32. "Fairfax County, Virginia."

33. Stephen Dillon, *Fugitive Life: The Queer Politics of the Prison State* (Durham, NC: Duke University Press, 2018), 130. Critical viewers may recognize, as we do, the irony in the contradiction the show presupposes between respectable viewers and the deviant predators. Most of the men who arrive at the bait house appear ordinary. We often learn, through their interrogations, that the "predators" are themselves fathers, brothers, and uncles—"seemingly honest and hardworking family men." As our colleague Alexandra Milla has noted in discussions of the program with one of us, the show might inadvertently expose a rot that exists at the heart of the cis-hetero-patriarchal order, a rot that has been historically "shielded from view by a veneer of social supremacy." Alexandra Milla, email to Paul Kaplan, April 8, 2021. In the next chapter, we read the show from the perspective of viewers who harbor their own anxieties about being able to discipline nonnormative desires.

34. *To Catch a Predator* periodically featured interviews with police officials who testified to the group's professionalism and reliability. In the Ocean County episode, for example, prosecutor Tom Kelleher "admits in the beginning he was concerned with working with Perverted Justice," Hansen explains in voice-over narration. The prosecutor then says, "We had heard some criticism from some official sources as a matter of fact. And that's why at first I was reluctant. But after we did our due diligence, I was satisfied to go ahead with it." Viewers learned that the group "met our standards" and provided the kind of labor that his understaffed computer sex crimes unit needed. "Ocean County, New Jersey: Part 1," episode 18 of *Dateline NBC: To Catch a Predator Special Report*, hosted by Chris Hansen, aired July 18, 2007, on MSNBC.

35. Content analyses of *Cops* in its early years reveal how the show invoked this mythology. The show focused disproportionately on violent crime, making the most fear-inducing forms of crime seem more prevalent than they actually were. Judith Newman, "Reality Check," *Adweek*, May 1992. And the culprits of that crime, moreover, were often nonwhite. When African Americans appeared on *Cops*, they were suspects 77% of the time. (By contrast, whites were suspects in just 38.4% of the show's vignettes.) Other studies showed that viewers were drawn to the show's punitive thrills. Researchers found that viewership of *Cops* and shows like it was significantly associated with higher levels of punitiveness and racism. Mary Beth Oliver and G. Blake Armstrong, "Predictors of Viewing and Enjoyment of Reality-Based and Fictional Crime Shows," *Journalism and Mass Communication Quarterly* 72, no. 3 (1995): 559–70. Authoritarianism among viewers, moreover, was positively associated with enjoyment of scenes portraying police use of force on criminal suspects, but only when the suspects were African American. Mary Beth Oliver, "Influences of Authoritarianism and Portrayals of Race on Caucasian Viewers' Responses to Reality-Based Crime Dramas," *Communication Reports* 9, no. 2 (1996): 141–50.

36. In her study of how the media covers the use of force by police officers, Regina Lawrence has demonstrated that "the typical news story about the use of force is brief, episodic, and structured around claims provided by police spokesmen and politicians. Crucially, these same sources usually 'individualize' police use of force, focusing public attention on deviant, violent criminal suspects who threaten officers and the public and, occasionally, on 'rogue cops' who lose control and cross the line between acceptable and unacceptable force. This

kind of coverage normalizes what some might call brutality and marginalizes competing perspectives on the existence of brutality problems and the causal roots of police violence." Regina Lawrence, *The Politics of Force: Media and the Construction of Police Brutality* (Berkeley: University of California Press, 2000), 34. Content analyses of *Cops* have shown that the officers portrayed on the show in its early years were overwhelmingly white, and they were more likely to use force on people of color than white suspects. Mary Beth Oliver, "Portrayals of Crime, Race, and Aggression in 'Reality-Based' Police Shows: A Content Analysis," *Journal of Broadcasting and Electronic Media* 38, no. 2 (1994): 179–92.

37. There is a growing literature on the history of policing in the United States. See, e.g., Marilynn S. Johnson, *Street Justice: A History of Police Violence in New York City* (Boston: Beacon Press, 2003); Jordan T. Camp and Christina Heatherton, eds., *Policing the Planet: Why the Policing Crisis Led to Black Lives Matter* (London: Verso Books, 2016); Andrea J. Ritchie, *Invisible No More: Police Violence Against Black Women and Women of Color* (Boston: Beacon Press, 2017); Carl Suddler, *Presumed Criminal: Black Youth and the Justice System in Postwar New York* (New York: NYU Press, 2019); Emily L. Thuma, *All Our Trials: Prisons, Policing, and the Feminist Fight to End Violence* (Urbana: University of Illinois Press, 2019); Stuart Schrader, *Badges Without Borders: How Global Counterinsurgency Transformed American Policing* (Berkeley: University of California Press, 2019); Max Felker-Kantor, *Policing Los Angeles: Race, Resistance, and the Rise of the LAPD* (Chapel Hill: University of North Carolina Press, 2018); Simon Balto, *Occupied Territory: Policing Black Chicago from Red Summer to Black Power* (Chapel Hill: University of North Carolina Press, 2019); and Elizabeth Hinton, *America on Fire: The Untold Story of Police Violence and Black Rebellion Since the 1960s* (New York: Liveright, 2021).

38. Elayne Rapping, "Aliens, Nomads, Mad Dogs, and Road Warriors: The Changing Face of Criminal Violence on TV," in *Reality TV: Remaking Television Culture*, ed. Susan Murray and Laurie Ouellette (New York: NYU Press, 2004), 218–19.

39. James Wolcott, "Car 54, Where Are You?" *New Yorker*, February 8, 1993.

40. Multiple histories and analyses of mass incarceration in the late twentieth century have espoused a view of the prison as a tool for managing volatile surplus labor. Consciously or unconsciously, these histories argue, neoliberal economic policies consigned many of the population's poor (and disproportionately Black) members to prisons while maintaining, in urban and exurban wastelands, a workforce to fill the needs of a service economy dependent on cheap labor. See, e.g., Ruth Wilson Gilmore, *Golden Gulag: Prisons, Surplus, Crisis, and Opposition in Globalizing California* (Berkeley: University of California Press, 2007); Loïc Wacquant, *Punishing the Poor: The Neoliberal Government of Social Insecurity* (Durham, NC: Duke University Press, 2009); and Dillon, *Fugitive Life*.

41. Criminologists have long described many of the criminal behaviors depicted in *Cops* as responses to structural impediments to well-being: the absence of good-paying jobs (the drug trade, theft), the stressors of poverty (drug addiction, domestic violence), and the unregulated competition within illegal economies (gang crime).

42. On cultural pathology and the late twentieth-century expansion of the carceral state, see Murakawa, *The First Civil Right*, and Hinton, *From the War on Poverty to the War on Crime*.

43. Philip Smith, *Punishment and Culture* (Chicago: University of Chicago Press, 2008), 43.

44. "Caught in a Lie Special Edition," season 25, episode 8 of *Cops*, executive produced by John Langley, aired February 9, 2013, on Paramount.

45. "Arrests with a Twist #2 Special Edition," season 24, episode 21 of *Cops*, executive produced by John Langley, aired March 31, 2012, on Paramount.

46. Glynn, *Tabloid Culture*, 41.

47. "Spinning Out," season 31,episode 21 of *Cops*, executive produced by John Langley, aired March 4, 2019, on Paramount.

48. Ibid.

49. Office of Policy Planning and Research, US Department of Labor, *The Negro Family: The Case for National Action* (Washington, DC: US Government Printing Office, 1965), https://www.dol.gov/general/aboutdol/history/webid-moynihan.

50. See, e.g., Patrick Fagan and Robert Rector, "How Welfare Harms Kids," The Heritage Foundation, June 5, 1996, https://www.heritage.org/welfare/report/how-welfare-harms-kids (accessed July 8, 2021).

51. The white, liberal embrace of this theory of Black pathology, recent scholarship has shown, infected efforts to eradicate poverty in the 1960s. Programs aimed at redressing inequality were quickly linked to crime prevention, which ultimately shifted their focus from providing opportunity to policing delinquency. Hinton, *From the War on Poverty to the War on Crime.*

52. Qtd. in John Larrabee, "Good 'Cops,' Bad 'Cops': Police on TV," *USA Today*, May 27, 1997.

53. Charles Lane, "Good Cops, Bad Cops," *New Republic*, April 3, 1995.

54. Kathleen Curry, "Mediating *Cops*: An Analysis of Viewer Reaction to Reality TV," *Journal of Criminal Justice and Popular Culture* 8 (2001): 169–85, 180. In that sense, the show supports theories by cultural criminologists about how popular culture works to generate widespread acquiescence to the violence of policing and punishment. It does so by inviting the viewers to see the criminal justice system as something "over there"—that is, a fundamental part of the political order that affects others' lives but not their own. Michelle Brown, *The Culture of Punishment: Prison, Society, and Spectacle* (New York: NYU Press, 2009).

55. On the culture wars of the 1980s and 1990s, see Andrew Hartman, *A War for the Soul of America*, 2nd ed. (Chicago: University of Chicago Press, 2019).

56. Heather Mason Kiefer, "Public on Justice System: Fair, but Still Too Soft," Gallup Organization, February 3, 2004, https://news.gallup.com/poll/10474/public-justice-system-fair-still-too-soft.aspx.

57. Martha C. Nussbaum, *Hiding from Humanity: Shame, Disgust, and the Law* (Princeton, NJ: Princeton University Press, 2004).

2. Watching the Night Creatures

1. "Drunk in Love," season 27, episode 27 of *Cops*, executive produced by John Langley, aired February 21, 2015, on Paramount.

2. For example, cops in LA investigating victims of the "Grim Sleeper" serial killer in the 1980s referred to the female drug users Lonnie Franklin killed as "nonhumans." Regina Austin, "Only 'Good Victims' Need Apply: 'Tales of the Grim Sleeper' and Poor Black Women in Crack Culture," *Docs and the Law Blog*, May 27, 2016, https://www.law.upenn.edu/live/news/6203-only-good-victims-need-apply-tales-of-the-grim#sthash.czI2gPHs.dpbs (accessed July 21, 2021). On Rodney King see Tracy Wood and Sheryl Stolberg, "Patrol Car Log in Beating Released," *Los Angeles Times*, March 19, 1991.

3. Michel Foucault, *Discipline and Punish: The Birth of the Prison* (Paris: Editions Gallimard, 1975);, English translation by. Alan Sheridan (New York: Vintage Books, 1995), 286. Citations refer to the Vintage edition.

4. Peter L. Berger and Thomas Luckmann, *The Social Construction of Reality: A Treatise in the Sociology of Knowledge* (New York: Anchor Books, 1967); David Garland, "The Limits of the Sovereign State: Strategies of Crime Control in Contemporary Society," *British Journal of Criminology* 36, no. 4 (1996): 445–71; and Ali Rattansi, *Bauman and Contemporary Sociology: A Critical Analysis* (Manchester: Manchester University Press, 2017).

5. Karin Brulliard, "Zookeeper Who Killed Tigers and Tried to Have Rival Murdered Is Sentenced to 22 Years in Prison," *Washington Post*, January 22, 2020.

6. *Oxford English Dictionary*, s.v. "ennui," https://www.oed.com/ (retrieved July 25, 2021). An unresolved or unresolvable question is whether boredom for human beings is historical or ahistorical; ideal or materialist? Put another way—does boredom precede and/or transcend human culture? See Elizabeth S. Goodstein, *Experience without Qualities: Boredom and Modernity* (Palo Alto, CA: Stanford University Press, 2005).

7. Kevin Aho, "Simmel on Acceleration, Boredom and Extreme Aesthesia," *Journal for the Theory of Social Behaviour* 37, no. 4 (2007): 447–62, 448.

8. Ibid.

9. John Lennon and Malcom Foley, *Dark Tourism: The Attraction of Death and Disaster* (New York: Continuum, 2000).

10. Qtd. in Jeff Ferrell, "Boredom, Crime, and Criminology," *Theoretical Criminology* (Special Issue on Cultural Criminology) 8, no. 3 (2004): 287–302, 291.

11. Aho, "Simmel on Acceleration," 455, 458.

12. Ferrell, "Boredom, Crime, and Criminology," 292, 289.

13. Raoul Vaneigem, *The Revolution of Everyday Life* (1967; London: Rebel Press, 2001); qtd. in Ferrell, "Boredom, Crime, and Criminology," 292.

14. Jack Katz, *Seductions of Crime: Moral and Sensual Attractions in Doing Evil* (New York: Basic Books, 1988), 301, italics in original.

15. Emilie Gomart and Antoine Hennion, "A Sociology of Attachment: Music, Amateurs, Drug Users," in *Actor Network Theory and After*, ed. John Law and John Hassard (Malden, MA: Blackwell Publishing, 1999), 226–27, italics in original.

16. Ibid., 235.

17. Qtd. in Ferrell, "Boredom, Crime, and Criminology," 292.

18. bell hooks, "Eating the Other: Desire and Resistance," in hooks, *Black Looks: Race and Representation* (Boston: South End Press, 1992), 21.

19. Ibid.

20. Kevin Drum, "A Very Brief History of Super Predators," *Mother Jones*, March 3, 2016, https://www.motherjones.com/kevin-drum/2016/03/very-brief-history-super-predators/.

21. On the construction of whiteness in mass culture, see Richard Dyer, *White: Essays on Race and Culture* (New York: Routledge, 1997).

22. Katz, *Seductions of Crime*, 8.

23. On the legal regulation of adolescent sexuality, see Carolyn Cocca, *Jailbait: The Politics of Statutory Rape Laws in the United States* (Albany: SUNY Press, 2004). Of course, the sexualization of adolescents is old news—the arena-rock band KISS had a huge hit in the 1970s called "Christine Sixteen." Plenty of twenty-first-century Instagram and TikTok viewers posing in nearly nude pictures and videos are minors. Popular search terms on pornographic websites such as Pornhub include "teen" and "step-daughter" and "boy." One satirical take on *To Catch a Predator*, a sketch on the television program *Mad TV*, sought laughs by featuring a man who is incapable of being shamed by Hansen, so confident is he that his attraction to underage teenagers is normal and shared by Hansen and other men. The sketch writers did, it is important to note, raise the age of the decoy to seventeen. But the larger point it was trying to make—that attraction to adolescents is not as abhorrent as the show suggests—still stands. Steven A. Kohm interprets the rise of satire and comedic tropes involving fictional characters being mistaken as pedophiles as a byproduct of the punitive culture that *To Catch a Predator* embodies. By showcasing "the dark side of society's impulse to utterly destroy putative or suspected pedophiles," he argues, the show "may have inadvertently tapped into latent societal fears of being erroneously or maliciously singled out for social expulsion." Kohm, "Representing the Pedophile," in *Routledge International Handbook of Visual Criminology*, ed. Michelle Brown and Eamonn Carrabine (New York: Routledge, 2017), 190–201, 198.

24. Kevin M. Williams, Barry S. Cooper, Teresa M. Howell, John C. Yuille, and Delroy L. Paulhus, "Inferring Sexually Deviant Behavior from Corresponding Fantasies: The Role of Personality and Pornography Consumption," *Criminal Justice and Behavior* 36, no. 2 (2009): 198–222, 205. We could not, interestingly, find survey research about sexual fantasies that distinguished between pedophilia and pederasty.

25. Natasha Knack, Dave Holmes, and J. Paul Fedoroff, "Motivational Pathways Underlying the Onset and Maintenance of Viewing Child Pornography on the Internet." *Behavioral Sciences and the Law* 38, no. 2 (2020): 100–116, 106. The evidence showing the presence and apparent growth of online underworlds for child pornography trafficking is anecdotal and relies on government reports on crimes and some self-reporting. Michael H. Keller and Gabriel J. X. Dance, "The Internet Is Overrun with Images of Child Sexual Abuse. What Went Wrong?" *New York Times*, September 29, 2019. Much more research is needed to understand the empirical truth about rates of child pornography access and viewership. Moreover, the processes by which people decide to seek, collect, and share illegal pornography are not well understood beyond correlation research that identifies risk factors or personality characteristics of offenders. See Maire Henshaw, James R. P. Ogloff, and Jonathan A. Clough, "Looking Beyond the Screen: A Critical Review of the Literature on the Online Child Pornography

Offender," *Sexual Abuse* 29, no. 5 (2017): 416–45 and Philip R. Magaletta, Erik Faust, William Bickart, and Alix M. McLearen, "Exploring Clinical and Personality Characteristics of Adult Male Internet-Only Child Pornography Offenders," *International Journal of Offender Therapy and Comparative Criminology* 58, no. 2 (2014): 137–53.

26. Samuel Ebersole and Robert Woods. "Motivations for Viewing Reality Television: A Uses and Gratifications Analysis," *Southwestern Mass Communication Journal* 23, no. 1 (2007): 23–42, 25.

27. "Dangerous Web," season 13, episode 3 of *Dateline NBC*, reported by Chris Hansen, aired November 11, 2004, on NBC.

28. Allen Salkin, "Website Hunts Pedophiles, and TV Goes Along," *New York Times*, December 13, 2006.

29. "Long Beach, California," episode 12 of *Dateline NBC: To Catch a Predator*, hosted by Chris Hansen, aired January 30, 2007, on MSNBC.

30. Ibid.

31. "Riverside County, California."

32. In one of the best-known episodes of *To Catch a Predator*, a man is caught again attempting to rendezvous with a minor the day after he is humiliated at the sting house. "Fairfax County, Virginia."

33. Ibid.

34. "Bowling Green, Kentucky," episode 20 of *Dateline NBC: To Catch a Predator*, reported by Chris Hansen, aired December 28, 2007, on MSNBC. In its first two iterations, *To Catch a Predator* was not working with police agencies, so the men were not immediately arrested outside the sting house.

35. David Savran, *Taking It Like a Man: White Masculinity, Masochism, and Contemporary American Culture* (Princeton, NJ: Princeton University Press, 1998), 27.

36. Ibid., 25.

37. Ibid., 10, 9. In the nineteenth century, Savran notes, Sigmund Freud pathologized the phenomenon, using the term "moral masochist" to describe a dysfunctional splitting of the male subject into conflicting male and female identities (the masculine superego and the feminized ego), a theory that was later used to explain homosexuality.

38. We are not the first to notice the masochistic qualities of *To Catch a Predator*. Mapping the show onto the three stages of masochistic fantasy detailed by Freud in "A Child Is Being Beaten," Amy Adler has offered a reading of the show as an "S/M scene," and has suggested that, beyond depicting the penal subject as masochistic, it invites the viewers to partake in its masochistic pleasure: "The show pictures the enthralled viewer as strangely complicit with the predator, imagining that we too will somehow delight, albeit under the veil of condemnation, in his fantasies." It also, she suggests, creates guilt and a desire to be punished that results from our enjoyment of the suspect's humiliation. Our work situates that masochism in the late modern criminological, penological, and political-economic context and suggests that it plays a role in the ongoing process of maintaining consent to punitive ideology that texts like *To Catch a Predator* engage in. Amy Adler, "*To Catch a Predator*," *Columbia Journal of Gender and Law* 21, no. 2 (2012): 130–58, 156.

39. While there are other "intoxisploitation" programs, such as *Drugs, Inc.* or *Celebrity Rehab*, *Intervention* is the first and longest running program in this subgenre.

40. Kelsey Osgood, "Has *Intervention* Become Too Ubiquitous for Its Own Good?" *Vulture*, March 23, 2015, https://www.vulture.com/2015/03/intervention-tv-too-ubiquitous-for-its-own-good.html, and Philiana Ng, "'Hoarders,' 'Intervention' Have Solid Returns on A&E," *Hollywood Reporter*, January 3, 2012, https://www.hollywoodreporter.com/live-feed/hoarders-intervention-have-solid-returns-277620.

41. Elizabeth Bernstein, *Temporarily Yours: Intimacy, Authenticity, and the Commerce of Sex* (Chicago: University of Chicago Press, 2007).

42. On repulsion/attraction, see William Ian Miller, *The Anatomy of Disgust* (Cambridge: Harvard University Press, 1998).

43. Moreover, the narrative structure is created by the producers of the show, who are thus inherently complicit in the exploitation of their subjects' addiction for the purposes of "good TV" and profit.

44. Jerome Bruner, "The Narrative Construction of Reality," *Critical Inquiry* 18, no. 1 (1991): 1–21.

45. Anthony G. Amsterdam and Jerome Bruner, *Minding the Law* (Cambridge: Harvard University Press, 2002), 113–14, italics in original.

46. Ibid., 121.

47. Patricia Ewick and Susan S. Silbey, "Subversive Stories and Hegemonic Tales: Toward a Sociology of Narrative," *Law and Society Review* 29, no. 2 (1995): 197–226, 197.

48. Jon Caramonica, "Addiction as High Drama," *Los Angeles Times*, December 17, 2006.

49. "Coley," season 3, episode 12 of *Intervention*, created by Sam Mettler, aired August 10, 2007, on A&E.

50. Virginia Heffernan, "Confronting a Crystal Meth Head Who Is Handy with a Chainsaw," *New York Times*, August 10, 2007.

51. "Katie S.," season 16, episode 2 of *Intervention*, created by Sam Mettler, aired November 29, 2007, on A&E.

52. Matthew Gilbert, "Vile 'Intervention' Pulls a Fast One," *Boston Globe*, March 5, 2005.

53. David Bianculli, "Badly in Need of Rehab: A&E's Series 'Intervention,'" *New York Daily News*, February 25, 2005.

54. Virginia Heffernan, "In Vino Veritas," *New York Times*, February 10, 2008.

55. Because *Intervention* is carefully edited, it is impossible to know how long the back-and-forth between the addict and the interventionist/family unit took, nor how many times the addict left and returned to the scene.

56. "Joey," season 6, episode 11 of *Intervention*, created by Sam Mettler, aired August 10, 2009, on A&E.

57. Philippe Bourgois and Jeffrey Schonberg, *Righteous Dopefiend* (Berkeley: University of California Press, 2009).

58. "Joey."

59. Osgood, "Has *Intervention* Become Too Ubiquitous for Its Own Good?"

60. The show's absolutism creates embarrassing moments of contradiction. It is so eager to get Joey, a man struggling with heroin addiction, on a plane to rehab that the producers had not planned for the necessity of mitigating the withdrawal symptoms that would make such a trip intolerable. To close the deal with him, they allow him to obtain and inject heroin before he enters detox.

61. Protesting a special series of episodes of *Intervention* that planned to focus on the drug epidemic afflicting Philadelphia's Kensington neighborhood, the manager of one of South Philadelphia's medication-assisted treatment centers noted that the show's approach ignores structural questions like "decades of disinvestment and the mass incarceration that devastated the neighborhood during the crack epidemic." Brooke Feldman told a local reporter, "You can't talk about the conditions in Kensington today without talking about the larger war on drugs and how these conditions were manufactured," . . . It's stigmatizing a community for being the symptom bearer of these larger issues." Aubrey Whelan, "Crisis in Hi-Def; Next Season of A&E's 'Intervention' Is Set in Philly: Is That a Good Thing?" *Philadelphia Daily News*, August 2, 2019.

62. Bianculli, "Badly in Need of Rehab"; Kevin Crust, "Giving Addicts a Jolt of Reality," *Los Angeles Times*, March 4, 2005; Gilbert, "Vile 'Intervention' Pulls a Fast One"; Lynn Smith, "Rehab: It's a Ripe Subject for Reality TV, but Does It Help or Exploit Addicts," *Calgary Herald* (Alberta, Canada), April 6, 2005; Amy Kaufman, "Exploiting Addicts? 'Celebrity Rehab' and 'Intervention' Raise Troubling Ethical Questions," *Philadelphia Daily News*, January 10, 2011.

63. In 2017 New Jersey politician Scott Rudder coined the phrase "the opioid-addiction industrial complex" to describe a nexus of pharmaceutical companies, addiction treatment centers, and prisons that profit from Americans' addiction to opiates. Scott Rudder, "Op-Ed: The Opioid-Addiction Industrial Complex—America's Dirty Secret," *NJ Spotlight*, May 24, 2017, https://www.njspotlight.com/2017/05/17-05-23-op-ed-the-opioid-addiction-industrial-complex-america-s-dirty-secret/. Rudder suggests that while the recent so-called opioid crisis has been catastrophic for addicts and their loved ones, it has reaped huge benefits for commercial and nonprofit entities delivering opioids and treatment to addicts. The addiction industrial complex's (AIC) constituent parts are persons, organizations, or spaces that benefit from addicts one way or another: drug manufacturers, traffickers, dealers, jails, courts, drug courts, prisons, detox centers, hospitals, residential rehab programs, outpatient rehab programs, sober living houses, 12-Step programs (AA and NA), and other (non–12-step based) recovery programs such as SMART Recovery. All of these feed on or service millions of addicts every day in the United States. Left off this list is the academic component of the AIC, where PhDs and MDs at universities, medical schools, and think tanks search for etiologies and treatments for the bio-psycho-social causes of addiction. The sum is an enormous and intricate network that constructs and feeds hegemonic concepts of "addiction" and "recovery" that generate folk and professional knowledge about intoxication, abstinence, human morality, and public policy.

64. See, e.g., "D'Amore Healthcare Featured in A&E's 'Intervention,'" *PR Newswire*, New York, January 17, 2018; "Luxury Rehab Center Airs Commercial During A&E's 'Intervention,'" *Presswire*, Coventry, July 22, 2016.

3. Cuffs of Love

1. "Limon, Colorado Extended Stay: Pain," episode 77 of *Lockup*, created by Rasha Drachkovitch, aired December 19, 2009, on MSNBC.

2. Ibid.

3. The most recent version of the *Lockup* style show is *60 Days In*, debuting on *A&E* in 2016. This iteration of the in-custody show follows volunteers as they attempt to navigate living inside a county jail for two months, ostensibly to observe the conditions and practices of inmates and staff.

4. David A. Green, "Penal Optimism and Second Chances: The Legacies of American Protestantism and the Prospects for Penal Reform," *Punishment and Society* 15, no. 2 (2013): 123–46.

5. Benjamin Rush, *Essays: Literary, Moral, and Philosophical*, ed. Michael Meranze (Schenectady, NY: Union College Press, 1988), 90; qtd. in Caleb Smith, *The Prison and the American Imagination* (New Haven, CT: Yale University Press, 2009), 47.

6. Ashley T. Rubin, *The Deviant Prison: Philadelphia's Eastern State Penitentiary and the Origins of America's Modern Penal System, 1829–1913* (New York: Cambridge University Press, 2021).

7. Smith, *The Prison and the American Imagination*, 6.

8. David Garland, *The Culture of Control: Crime and Social Order in Contemporary Society* (Chicago: University of Chicago Press, 2001), and Joachim J. Savelsberg, Lara L. Cleveland, and Ryan D. King, "Institutional Environments and Scholarly Work: American Criminology, 1951–1993," *Social Forces* 82, no. 4 (2004): 1275–1302. One of the most dramatic moments in this change occurred in 1974 when criminologists Douglas Lipton, Robert Martinson, and Judith Wilks published what Martinson had famously distilled for a wider audience in a 1974 article in *Public Interest*. The researchers had surveyed 231 rehabilitation programs and found that they had no discernable influence, positive or negative, on recidivism rates. Journalists summed up the study, later called "the most politically influential criminological study of the last half century," with the phrase "Nothing Works." Robert Martinson, "What Works: Questions and Answers about Prison Reform," *The Public Interest* 35 (Spring 1974): 22–54.

9. Aaron Griffith, *God's Law and Order: The Politics of Punishment in Evangelical America* (Cambridge, MA: Harvard University Press, 2020).

10. Jack Curry, "MSNBC's Incarceration Series Has Lock on Ratings," *Washington Post*, July 10, 2011.

11. Garland, *The Culture of Control*, 184.

12. "Hackensack Extended Stay: Thicker than a Bowl of Oatmeal," episode 179 of *Lockup*, created by Rasha Drachkovitch, aired March 1, 2014, on MSNBC.

13. "Long Island Extended Stay: Red and Whites," episode 213 of *Lockup*, created by Rasha Drachkovitch, aired June 27, 2015, on MSNBC.

14. "Inside Folsom Prison," episode 17 of *Lockup*, created by Rasha Drachkovitch, aired January 28, 2006, on MSNBC.

15. "Orange County Jail Extended Stay: The Confession," episode 104 of *Lockup*, created by Rasha Drachkovitch, aired December 25, 2010, on MSNBC.

16. "Hackensack Extended Stay: Thicker than a Bowl of Oatmeal."

17. Existing scholarship on *Lockup* and other like shows emphasizes these pessimistic portrayals of inmates. In a content analysis of *Lockup*, criminologists Dawn K. Cecil and Jennifer L. Leitner demonstrate its producers' fixation on danger and security. The show focuses on large, maximum-security facilities; it overstates the risk of assault inmates face; it disproportionately represents men in the position of guards; and it dwells on inmates who are in solitary confinement, known as "the hole" or "ad-seg" (administrative segregation) and those serving long sentences. As a result, they argue that inmates appear as fearsome others. Dawn K. Cecil and Jennifer L. Leitner, "Unlocking the Gates: An Examination of *MSNBC Investigates—Lockup*," *Howard Journal of Criminal Justice* 48, no. 2 (March 2009): 184–99. In the same vein, cultural studies scholar John Riofrio notes a connection between the show's fixation on the bodies of inmates and its constant warnings about how dangerous they are, arguing that the show serves as a "means of assuring our own control over a social group that we don't understand, that we actively fear and yet find intriguing." John Riofrio, "Spectacles of Incarceration: Ideological Violence in Prison Documentaries," *symplokē* 20, nos. 1–2 (2012): 139–52, 151. Communication scholar Elizabeth Barfoot Christian has noted the degree to which *Louisiana Lockdown*, a *Lockup* knockoff, trafficked in "displays of humiliation," arguing that the "cumulative effect of this television genre will be an increasing dehumanization in our punishment of all those accused and convicted of crimes." We argue that these interpretations miss the humanizing, optimistic moments in these programs and miss, in turn, the way that humanization can and does work, paradoxically, to justify harsh, "inhumane" treatment. "Are you ready for your 15 minutes of shame? *Louisiana Lockdown* and Narrative in Prison Reality Television," in *Reality Television: Oddities of Culture*, ed. Alison F. Slade, Amber J. Narro, and Burton P. Buchanan (Lanham, MD.: Lexington Books, 2014), 59–76, 74.

18. David Hinckley, "A Barbaric Life Behind Bars," *New York Daily News*, July 5, 2008.

19. "Limon, Colorado Extended Stay: Pain."

20. Cecil and Leitner, "Unlocking the Gates," 193. We also note the sexual desire these shows cultivate of inmates' "dangerous" bodies. Shots in prisons often depict inmates shirtless, working out at the gym, and so on, giving an erotic charge to these scenes. James Parker's article in *The Atlantic*, titled "prison porn," captures how the shows blur the lines between phobia and fetish in their "thrilling," "tickling" depictions of "*hard* surfaces, *hard* voices, *hard* lights; the big dude hanging heavy forearms over the back of a chair as he tells his tale; the hellishly perfected torsos around the weights bench, where a scowling lifter struts like the creature in William Blake's *The Ghost of a Flea*." James Parker, "Prison Porn," *The Atlantic* (March 2010): 36–37, 37 (emphasis added).

21. "Inside Utah State Prison," episode 4 of *Lockup*, created by Rasha Drachkovitch, aired June 25, 2005, on MSNBC.

22. "Inside Folsom Prison."

23. "County Jail," season 2, episode 6 of *Lockdown*, directed by David Ross Smith, aired March 23, 2008, on National Geographic Channel. This refusal to be reduced to a number evokes the men in prison films of the early twentieth century who heroically maintain their dignity in the most trying conditions. Nicole Rafter, *Shots in the Mirror: Crime Films and Society*, 2nd ed. (New York: Oxford University Press, 2006).

24. "Return to Valley State," episode 2 of *Lockup*, created by Rasha Drachkovitch, aired June 11, 2005, on MSNBC.

25. "Inmate University," season 2, episode 4 of *Lockdown*, directed by David Ross Smith, aired October 28, 2007, on National Geographic Channel.

26. "Inside the Kill Fence," season 5, episode 3 of *Lockdown*, directed by David Ross Smith, aired January 10, 2010, on National Geographic Channel.

27. "Return to Valley State."

28. "Return to Pelican Bay," episode 8 of *Lockup*, created by Rasha Drachkovitch, aired July 23, 2005, on MSNBC.

29. We draw here from work by Patricia Ewick and Susan S. Silbey on the sociology of narrative. Hegemonic stories, they argue, "emphasize particularity" and "efface the connection between the particular and the general." Patricia Ewick and Susan S. Silbey, "Subversive Stories and Hegemonic Tales: Toward a Sociology of Narrative," *Law and Society Review* 29, no. 2 (1995): 197–226, 200.

30. Programs such as *Lockup* bracket out not only the large structural forces that help explain macro-level problems like poverty and educational opportunity, but also any kind of sophisticated micro-level analysis of the significance of power and storytelling by vulnerable persons like prisoners. As anthropologists Philippe Bourgois and Jeffrey Schonberg show in their ethnography of homeless heroin addicts, some men who are addicted and living on the streets claim to be veterans of overseas combat, having never been deployed, in order create a sympathetic and charismatic self-narrative that resonates with listeners and in some sense absolves them of guilt over their dire situations. See Philippe Bourgois and Jeffrey Schonberg, *Righteous Dopefiend* (Berkeley: University of California Press, 2009).

31. "County Jail."

32. Tom Jackman, "*Lockup* Off to Solid Start in Portraying Life in Fairfax County Jail," *Washington Post*, September 8, 2014.

33. Eileen R. Meehan, "God, Capitalism, and the Family Dog." In *A Companion to Reality Television*, ed. Laurie Ouellette (Malden, MA: Wiley Blackwell, 2014), 171–88, 180.

34. "Dog the Bounty Hunter Scores in Ratings," Reuters News Service, January 27, 2001, https://www.reuters.com/article/television-viewers-bountyhunter-idUK-TRE70Q96520110127 (accessed September 14, 2020). The show even survived a scandal in season 4 when leaked recordings of Chapman using the n-word in taped telephone conversations with his son led A&E to cancel the show, only to bring it back after a massive campaign by viewers to reinstate the show succeeded. Shelley Fralic, "After *Dog*, Duane Chapman Wants to Be Criminal Justice Czar," *Vancouver Sun*, July 18, 2009.

35. As historian Aaron Griffith explains, that response was complex. Since the 1970s evangelicals "not only lobbied for policies and voted for politicians who helped build America's carceral state, they also helped make these changes appealing to other citizens." And yet their missionary work in prisons also made them "pioneers in humanitarian engagement with modern prison life." Their concern with the spiritual conversion of inmates sometimes "offered cover for punitive politics, but other times conversion opened Evangelicals' eyes to the needs of juvenile delinquents and prisoners, leading them to solidarity with offenders and new forms of reform work. Griffith, *God's Law and Order*, 3–4.

36. "Interview with Dog the Bounty Hunter," *Montel Williams Show*, executive produced by Montel Williams and Diane Rappoport, aired September 5, 2005, in broadcast syndication.

37. The second half of the twentieth century had seen the dramatic growth of Evangelical Christianity in the United States. By the time the Evangelical Dog went on the air in 2004, the percentage of Americans who described themselves as "born again" or Evangelical stood at 43%. Frank Newport, "Five Things to Know about Evangelicals in America," *Gallup*, May 31, 2018, https://news.gallup.com/opinion/polling-matters/235208/things-know-evangelicals-america.aspx (accessed September 14, 2020). Evangelical Christians oppose the secularization and liberalization of culture (including the culture of mainline Protestant churches) while embracing the importance of individual lives being rooted in a moment of conversion to Christ.

38. Ibid.

39. Mary Douglas, *Purity and Danger: An Analysis of Concepts of Pollution and Taboo* (New York: Routledge and Kegan Paul, 1966), 35.

40. "Suga on My Cuffs," season 2, episode 21 of *Dog the Bounty Hunter*, aired November 29, 2005. All episodes of *Dog the Bounty Hunter* were produced by Daniel Elias, David Houts, David McKillop, and Neil A. Cohen and appeared on A&E.

41. "Meet the Chapmans," season 1, episode 1 of *Dog the Bounty Hunter*, aired August 30, 2004.

42. "Make a Wish," season 4, episode 3 of *Dog the Bounty Hunter*, aired April 24, 2007.

43. "Bait and Snitch," season 6, episode 17 of *Dog the Bounty Hunter*, aired April 21, 2010.

44. Tanya Erzen, "Testimonial Politics: The Christian Right's Faith-Based Approach to Marriage and Imprisonment," *American Quarterly* 59, no. 3 (2007): 991–1015.

45. "Make a Wish."

46. Moreover, Dog's investment in this theory of human reformation corresponds to concepts of recovery from addiction that flourished during the rise of neoliberalism in the 1980s. While Nancy Reagan was exhorting the nation's youth to "just say no," counselors in "therapeutic community" residential rehabilitation centers, such as The Phoenix House, were employing a "tough love" type of therapy. This approach entailed breaking down the addict's sense of self through hierarchical discipline, manual labor, head shaving, community humiliation (e.g., requiring a resident who broke a rule to wear a cardboard sign displaying his or her transgression), and confrontational "encounter groups." Alex Mold and Virginia Berridge, *Voluntary Action and Illegal Drugs: Health and Society in Britain Since the 1960s*

(New York: Palgrave Macmillan, 2010), 29. Like Dog's philosophy of incarceration, tough love approaches to addiction treatment correspond to the myth of death and rebirth that, we have seen, underlie the earliest conceptions of the penitentiary.

47. Meehan, "God, Capitalism, and the Family Dog," 180.

48. Jonathan Drimmer, "When Man Hunts Man: The Rights and Duties of Bounty Hunters in the American Criminal Justice System," *University of Houston Law Review* 33, no. 3 (1996): 731–93, 733–34. Early treatment of the bail bondsmen in United States jurisprudence likened their relationship to defendants to that of masters to slaves. *Johnson v. Tompkins*, 13 F. Cas. 840 (C.C.E.D. Pa. 1833) (No. 7,416); cited in Drimmer, "When Man Hunts Man," 751 n. 117.

49. Ruth Wilson Gilmore, *Golden Gulag: Prisons, Surplus, Crisis, and Opposition in Globalizing California* (Berkeley: University of California Press, 2007), and Loïc Wacquant, *Punishing the Poor: The Neoliberal Government of Social Insecurity* (Durham, NC: Duke University Press, 2009); Malcolm M. Feeley and Jonathan Simon, "The New Penology: Notes on the Emerging Strategy of Corrections and Its Implications," *Criminology* 30, no. 4 (1992): 449–74.

50. "The Hunt for Santa," season 6, episode 4 of *Dog the Bounty Hunter*, aired December 23, 2009.

51. Qtd. in Meehan, "God, Capitalism, and the Family Dog," 185.

52. "Make a Wish."

53. "Best Of," season 7, episode 14 of *Dog the Bounty Hunter* aired January 26, 2011.

54. Meehan, "God, Capitalism, and the Family Dog," 175.

55. "Burn and Return," season 5, episode 6 of *Dog the Bounty Hunter*, aired August 20, 2008.

56. "You Can't Go Home Again," season 1, episode 12 of *Dog the Bounty Hunter*, aired November 8, 2004.

57. "Bustin' with Justin," season 3, episode 17 of *Dog the Bounty Hunter*, aired August 15, 2006.

58. Grace Elizabeth Hale, *A Nation of Outsiders: How the White Middle Class Fell in Love with Rebellion in Postwar America* (New York: Oxford University Press, 2011).

59. "Best Of."

60. Philip Smith, *Punishment and Culture* (Chicago: University of Chicago Press, 2008), 171.

61. Kevin M. Carlsmith, "The Roles of Retribution and Utility in Determining Punishment," *Journal of Experimental Social Psychology* 42, no. 4 (2006): 437–51.

62. Kevin M. Carlsmith et al., "The Paradoxical Consequences of Revenge," *Journal of Personality and Social Psychology* 95, no. 6 (2008): 1316–24. One 2008 study "found that participants who punished were actually less satisfied than those who did not punish and also ruminated more about the wrongdoer. Crucially, none of the participants expected this lack of satisfaction; they inaccurately expected that getting back at the offender would be satisfying." A critique of this study noted, however, that the experimenters had not investigated whether the outcome was linked to the absence, in the experiment, of an opportunity for

the punished to provide feedback to the punisher acknowledging the punishment (ibid.). Study finding paraphrased in Friederike Funk, Victoria McGeer, and Mario Gollwitzer, "Get the Message: Punishment Is Satisfying if the Transgressor Responds to Its Communicative Intent," *Personality and Social Psychology Bulletin* 40, no. 8 (2014): 986–97, 987.

63. Funk, McGeer, and Gollwitzer, "Get the Message." The architects of premodern executions may have intuitively understood this dynamic. As part of the execution ritual, "the law required that its victim should authenticate in some sense the tortures that he had undergone." Michel Foucault, *Discipline and Punish: The Birth of the Prison* (Paris: Editions Gallimard, 1975), trans. Alan Sheridan (New York: Vintage Books, 1995), 66. Citations refer to the Vintage edition.

64. On the decline of punishment's symbolic and expressive functions in the age of mass incarceration see Patricia Ewick, "The Return of Restraint: Limits to the Punishing State," *Quinnipiac Law Review* 31, no. 3 (2013): 577–98.

65. Smith, *The Prison and the American Imagination*, 208.

66. Bill Nichols, *Introduction to Documentary*, 2nd ed. (Bloomington: Indiana University Press, 2010), 69.

67. Brett Story, Director's Statement, https://www.prisonlandscapes.com/directors-statement/ (accessed March 7, 2019).

68. Brett Story, "Against a 'Humanizing' Prison Cinema," in *Routledge International Handbook of Visual Criminology*, ed. Michelle Brown and Eamonn Carrabine (New York: Routledge, 2017), 455–65, 458, 459.

69. Story, "Against a 'Humanizing' Prison Cinema," 457.

70. Thomas B. Edsall, "The Expanding World of Poverty Capitalism," *New York Times*, August 26, 2014.

71. Story, "Against a 'Humanizing' Prison Cinema," 457.

4. Middlebrow Crimesploitation

1. Brenna Ehrlich, "Five Biggest Moments of 2010s' True-Crime Boom," *Rolling Stone*, December 27, 2019, https://www.rollingstone.com/culture/culture-features/2010s-true-crime-boom-podcasts-931441/.

2. Gray Cavender and Mark Fishman, "Television Reality Crime Programs: Context and History," in *Entertaining Crime: Television Reality Programs*, ed. Mark Fishman and Gray Cavender (New York: Walter de Gruyter, 1998), 3–15, 6.

3. Steven A. Kohm, "The People's Law versus Judge Judy Justice: Two Models of Law in American Reality-Based Courtroom TV," *Law and Society Review* 40, no. 3 (2006): 693–728, 708, 717, 708.

4. The term "middlebrow" generally refers to the tastes of middle-class consumers. While it is sometimes used pejoratively to describe the watering down of elite cultural forms for consumption by middle class audiences, we use it as one of its original users did in 1933. Writing in the *Saturday Review of Literature*, Margaret Widdemer described as middlebrow the "men and women, fairly civilized, fairly literate, who support the critics and lecturers and publishers by purchasing their wares." Quoting Widdemer, Joan Shelly Rubin explains

that such consumers were "located between the 'tabloid addict class' and the 'tiny group of intellectuals.'" Joan Shelley Rubin, *The Making of Middlebrow Culture* (Chapel Hill: University of North Carolina Press, 1992), xii–xiii.

5. Kevin Glynn, *Tabloid Culture: Trash Taste, Popular Power, and the Transformation of American Television* (Durham, NC: Duke University Press, 2000), 6.

6. Ibid.

7. On the "alternative trial" in fictional and nonfictional film, see Ticien Marie Sassoubre, "Knowing It When We See It: Realism and Melodrama in American Film Since *The Birth of a Nation*," in *Trial Films on Trial: Law, Justice, and Popular Culture*, ed. Austin Sarat, Martha Merrill Umphrey, and Jessica Silbey (Tuscaloosa: University of Alabama Press, 2019), 39–80.

8. David Garland, *The Culture of Control: Crime and Social Order in Contemporary Society* (Chicago: University of Chicago Press, 2001).

9. "Fighting for Their Lives," season 1, episode 10 of *Making a Murderer*, directed by Laura Ricciardi and Moira Demos, aired December 18, 2015, on Netflix, https://www.netflix.com/title/80000770 .

10. In an interview, Ricciardi argued that the question the series was asking was not "if Steven was guilty or innocent" but "how was he treated as the accused?" She explained, "We had chosen Steven's story because of his unique status as a DNA exoneree charged with a crime—this was an incredible opportunity to meet a man who was unequivocally failed by the system in 1985, and now was going to step back into it. Between '85–'05 there had been major advances in DNA, and huge legislative reform in the USA about police practices and investigative techniques. There was a lot of chat about wrongful convictions being a problem from the '80s and that 'we've advanced techniques, we're in the modern world and don't have these problems.' Well, we could test that. We were pointing our cameras at the prosecution." And yet the context Ricciardi discusses in this brief interview is surprisingly absent from the series, which makes no effort to connect the particulars in the case to this history of reform in the criminal justice system. Thomas Smith, "'It didn't matter to us if Steven was guilty or innocent': *Making A Murderer* Directors on Crafting Part 2," *New Musical Express*, October 22, 2018, https://www.nme.com/blogs/tv-blogs/making-a-murderer-part-2–2391632.

11. Charles D. Weisselberg, "Against Innocence," in *The Integrity of Criminal Process: From Theory to Practice*, ed. Jill Hunter, Paul Roberts, Simon N. M. Young, and David Dixon (Oxford: Hart Publishing, 2016), 349–70; Abbe Smith, "In Praise of the Guilty Project: A Criminal Defense Lawyer's Growing Anxiety about Innocence Projects," *University of Pennsylvania Journal of Law and Social Change* 13, no. 3 (2009–10): 315–30; Simon A. Cole and Jay D. Aronson, "Blinded by Science on the Road to Abolition?" in *The Road to Abolition? The Future of Capital Punishment in the United States*, ed. Charles Ogletree and Austin Sarat (New York: NYU Press, 2009); and Carol S. Steiker and Jordan M. Steiker, "The Seduction of Innocence: The Attractions and Limitations of the Focus on Innocence in Capital Punishment Law and Advocacy," *Journal of Criminal Law and Criminology* 95, no. 2 (2005): 587–624.

12. Robert J. Norris, *Exonerated: A History of the Innocence Movement* (New York: NYU Press, 2017), 177.

13. Carl Suddler, *Presumed Criminal: Black Youth and the Justice System in Postwar New York* (New York: NYU Press, 2019); Smith, "In Praise of the Guilty Project." Efforts to introduce new punitive measures have been sold on their sensitivity to popular concern about the harm the criminal justice system can do to innocent people. A failed effort to reinstate the death penalty in Massachusetts in 2005 was made with proposed legislation that would have made a death sentence contingent on the existence of DNA evidence linking the defendant to the capital crime. In 2016 Californians passed, by voter referendum, Proposition 66, a measure that speeds up the capital appeals process in order to hasten executions. There, too, the rights of the innocent are distinguished from the rights of the guilty: "A stay of execution shall not be granted for the purpose of considering a successive or untimely petition *unless the court finds that the petitioner has a substantial claim of actual innocence or ineligibility.*" Death Penalty Reform and Saving Act of 2016 (emphasis added), https://www.oag.ca.gov/system/files/initiatives/pdfs/15–0096%20(Death%20Penalty)_0.pdf (accessed September 13, 2016).

14. See, e.g., Sharon Dolovich, "Cruelty, Prison Conditions, and the Eighth Amendment," *NYU Law Review* 84, no. 4 (2009): 881–979; Colin Dayan, *The Story of Cruel and Unusual* (Cambridge, MA: MIT Press, 2007), and Keramet Reiter, *23/7: Pelican Bay Prison and the Rise of Long-Term Solitary Confinement* (New Haven, CT: Yale University Press, 2016).

15. Peter Brooks, *The Melodramatic Imagination: Balzac, Henry James, Melodrama, and the Mode of Excess* (New Haven, CT: Yale University Press, 1976).

16. In an interview, filmmaker Demos acknowledged the appeal to audiences of an "underdog" protagonist and his family, "victims of a system intended to overwhelm them. 'I think most people feel like underdogs in their lives,' Demos says. 'They feel like everything's against them, they want fairness. So this is something that people can latch on to.'" Michael Idato, "Shooting a Murder," *Sydney Morning Herald*, February 20, 2016.

17. On the history of cultural constructions of poor white people as "trash," see Nancy Isenberg, *White Trash: The 400-Year Untold History of Class in America* (New York: Viking Press, 2016).

18. Edward Wasserman, "Ethics of Poverty Coverage," *Journal of Mass Media Ethics* 28, no. 2 (2013): 138–40, 138.

19. Grace Elizabeth Hale, *A Nation of Outsiders: How the White Middle Class Fell in Love with Rebellion in Postwar America* (Oxford: Oxford University Press, 2011), 3.

20. "Indefensible," season 1, episode 4 of *Making a Murderer*, directed by Laura Ricciardi and Moira Demos, aired December 18, 2015, on Netflix, https://www.netflix.com/title/80000770.

21. Ibid.

22. Scott D. Pierce, "'Making a Murderer' Is Not about Avery's Guilt or Innocence," *Salt Lake Tribune*, January 21, 2016. "Our hope is the dialogue reaches beyond these cases or beyond Manitowoc County or Wisconsin, for that matter. This is an American story. This just happened to be a high-profile case that two filmmakers spent a decade chronicling so that people could see it in depth. But I guarantee you that what you see playing out in this series is playing out in every state in this nation, and there's a broader dialogue that needs to be happening." Daniel Holloway, "'Making a Murderer' Filmmakers Fire Back at

Prosecutor: 'He's Not Entitled to His Own Facts,'" *The Wrap*, December 31, 2015, https://www.thewrap.com/making-a-murderer-filmmakers-fire-back-at-prosecutor-hes-not-entitled-to-his-own-facts/ (accessed July 16, 2021).

23. As of April 30, 2016, the post had earned 5,657 "upvotes" and 409 responses from users. Our analysis of a single discussion thread on a single website is not intended to support the argument that *Making a Murderer* has a singular ideological effect on viewers (even most viewers), or that audiences monolithically "receive" texts in similar ways. Proceeding deductively and "cherry picking" our evidence, we present what follows in order to demonstrate the *possibility*, rather than the certainty, that these texts can reinforce the foundations of a broader punitive perspective of the world, even in those who may see themselves as sympathetic to a more liberal perspective on criminal justice policy. For an exploration of a wider range of emotions the series elicited from viewers on Reddit, see Liam Kennedy, 2018, "'Man I'm all torn up inside': Analyzing Audience Responses to *Making a Murderer*," *Crime, Media, Culture* 14, no. 3: 391–408.

24. Reddit Users, *Making a Murderer* Forum, "Can We Pause to Applaud Two of the Best Lawyers in the USA?" https://www.reddit.com/r/MakingaMurderer/comments/3z1000/can_we_pause_to_applaud_two_of_the_best_lawyers/ (accessed July 12, 2017), Copies of the text also on file with the authors.

25. Ibid.

26. Ibid.

27. Ibid.

28. Naomi Murakawa, *The First Civil Right: How Liberals Built Prison America* (New York: Oxford University Press, 2014), 43.

29. Marie Gottschalk, "The Long Shadow of the Death Penalty: Mass Incarceration, Capital Punishment, and Penal Policy in the United States," in *Is the Death Penalty Dying? European and American Perspectives*, ed. Austin Sarat and Jürgen Martschukat (New York: Cambridge University Press, 2011), 292–321.

30. "The Last Person to See Teresa Alive," season 1, episode 5 of *Making a Murderer*, directed by Laura Ricciardi and Moira Demos, aired December 18, 2015, on Netflix, https://www.netflix.com/title/80000770.

31. Reddit Users, *Making a Murderer* Forum.

32. Monica Davey, "Netflix Viewers Streaming Fury into Wisconsin," *New York Times*, January 29, 2016. Other reviewers responded to the series in a more vigilante fashion, harassing and threatening the Manitowoc County Sheriff's Department and key state figures in the series like Ken Kratz and Lieutenant Andrew Colborn, who told reporters that "Avery sympathizers have confronted him in public, threatened to kidnap and sodomize him and gang rape his wife, and have posted pictures of his children online." In December 2019 Colborn sued the filmmakers and Netflix for defamation. Rebecca Keegan, "Inside a 'Making a Murderer' Lawsuit and the Hidden Dangers of TV's True-Crime Craze," *Hollywood Reporter*, January 17, 2019.

33. Sometimes, as in *Making a Murderer*, "sleuthing" is literal, in the sense of searching for "the real killer"; in other instances, sleuthing is more about trying to understand the motivations of bad actors or the failures of systems.

34. Qtd. in Lynette Rice, "TV's Crime Spree," *Entertainment Weekly*, January 22, 2016, 19.

35. Alan H. Goldman, "The Appeal of the Mystery," *Journal of Aesthetics and Art Criticism* 69, no. 3 (2011), 261–72, 263–64.

36. Ibid, 268, 271.

37. State of Massachusetts, "Drug Lab Cases Information," https://www.mass.gov/info-details/drug-lab-cases-information (accessed July 15, 2021).

38. Ibid.

39. By meso level, we mean institutional. In other words, the critique that emerges on *How to Fix a Drug Scandal* is not of the large picture of oppression in relation to criminal justice in the United States (macro), but in terms of technical-legal failures in the specific liberal legal criminal justice system of two cities in Massachusetts.

40. Episode 2 of *How to Fix a Drug Scandal*, https://www.netflix.com/title/80233339. All episodes cited were directed and produced by Erin Lee Carr and appeared on Netflix on April 1, 2020.

41. Ibid

42. Episode 3 of *How to Fix a Drug Scandal*, https://www.netflix.com/title/80233339.

43. Episode 4 of *How to Fix a Drug Scandal*, https://www.netflix.com/title/80233339.

44. The docuseries makes one concrete suggestion: mandatory drug testing for forensic chemists.

45. Moreover, the show's aesthetic choices sometimes resemble those of exploitative tabloid television programs. Its introductory montage weaves together images of a razor cutting powder lines, shards of crystal, a lighter cooking a drug spoon, chunks of what looks like crack, pills, bags of powder and crystals, and smoke, along with one very brief image of what look like legal documents in stacks. A trip-hop track accompanies the fetishistic montage, advertising the contents of the program that follows as that which will titillate and excite. What follows is sometimes redolent of the gaze that is cast upon the subjects of lowbrow crimesploitation programs like *Intervention*. Peppered throughout *How to Fix a Drug Scandal* are dramatic re-enactments of Sonja Farak using drugs, blurring the lines between reality and fiction in tabloidesque form. The gratuitous reenactments of the crimes appeal to the broader desire to step into the experience of the criminal that we discussed in chapter 2—a desire that the show satisfies by exploiting the experience of a person whose life was ruined by drug abuse. A similar sort of dynamic characterizes the way the series dramatizes the cat-and-mouse pursuit of Farak. The producers cast an actor to play Farak who so closely resembles her that it becomes near impossible for the viewer to distinguish between actual recordings of interrogations of Farak and reenactments. The re-creation of these scenes shifts the show's focus from analysis to entertainment, which in turn places the viewer at a greater remove from the story being told. In reenactments, they become passive consumers of a juicy scandal rather than citizens gaining an understanding of how and why systems fail to protect the rights of criminal defendants.

46. Another recent middlebrow crimesploitation release from Netflix is *The Trials of Gabriel Fernandez* (2020). This six-episode serial explores the death of an eight-year-old boy from Palmdale, California, east of Los Angeles, who died from extreme abuse at the

hands of his mother and her boyfriend, both of whom were convicted of first-degree murder (Mahita Gajanan, "The Heartbreaking Story Behind Netflix's Documentary Series *The Trials of Gabriel Fernandez*," *Time*, March 3, 2020, https://time.com/5790549/gabriel-fernandez-netflix-documentary/). The serial focuses on the twin mysteries of how local social services failed to protect the boy, and the inexplicable horror of his parents' abuse of him, resulting in a show that is both about individual moral culpability and the failure of meso-level institutions.

47. James Pinkerton, "Seven Years after Scandal, Backlog Still Plagues HPD Crime Lab," *Houston Chronicle*, October 4, 2011; Rebecca McCray, "Jeff Sessions' Rejection of Science Leaves Local Prosecutors in the Dark," *Slate*, June 7, 2017, https://slate.com/news-and-politics/2017/06/disbanding-the-ncfs-will-lead-to-worse-outcomes.html.

48. Committee on Identifying the Needs of the Forensic Sciences Community, National Research Council, *Strengthening Forensic Science in the United States: A Path Forward* (Washington, DC: National Academy of Science, 2009), https://www.ncjrs.gov/pdffiles1/nij/grants/228091.pdf (accessed July 15, 2021).

49. McCray, "Jeff Sessions' Rejection of Science."

50. See, e.g., William Haltom and Michael McCann, *Distorting the Law: Politics, Media, and the Litigation Crisis* (Chicago: University of Chicago Press, 2004).

51. "Cat and Mouse," episode 1 of *Don't F**k with Cats: Hunting an Internet Killer*, directed by Mark Lewis, aired December 18, 2019, on Netflix, https://www.netflix.com/title/81031373.

52. Other recent Netflix true crime serials are whodunits, such as *Murder Mountain* (2018), which investigates the killing of a young man working in the marijuana industry in Humboldt, California.

53. Winston Ross, "Canada's 'Cannibal Killer': Early Reports Warned about Luka Magnotta," *Daily Beast*, July 13, 2017, https://www.thedailybeast.com/canadas-cannibal-killer-early-reports-warned-about-luka-magnotta.

54. "Closing the Net," episode 3 of *Don't F**k with Cats: Hunting an Internet Killer*, directed by Mark Lewis, aired December 18, 2019, on Netflix, https://www.netflix.com/title/81031373.

55. Ibid.

56. Patricia Ewick and Susan S. Silbey, "Subversive Stories and Hegemonic Tales: Toward a Sociology of Narrative," *Law and Society Review* 29, no. 2 (1995): 197–226.

57. Jonathan Simon, *Governing Through Crime: How the War on Crime Transformed American Democracy and Created a Culture of Fear* (New York: Oxford University Press, 2007).

58. Keith A. Findley, "'Making a Murderer' Shows That Our Justice System Needs a Healthy Dose of Humility," *Washington Post*, January 15, 2016.

59. Ibid.

60. Murakawa, *The First Civil Right*.

61. See, e.g., Dolovich, "Cruelty, Prison Conditions, and the Eighth Amendment"; Dayan, *The Story of Cruel and Unusual*; and Reiter, *23/7*.

62. Critical criminologists and historians have amassed a scholarly literature that charts that deep structure, from nuanced ethnographic studies of vulnerable populations

dwelling in the shadows of late capitalism (Philippe I. Bourgois and Jeffrey Schonberg, *Righteous Dopefiend* [Berkeley: University of California Press, 2009]), to arguments about contemporary systemic racism (Michelle Alexander, *The New Jim Crow: Incarceration in the Age of Colorblindness* [New York: The New Press, 2010]), to calls for prison abolition (Angela Davis, *Are Prison Obsolete?* [New York: Seven Stories Press, 2003]). Moreover, cultural criminologists have identified an array of understandable and engaging practices undertaken by marginalized persons, activists, and other nonacademics that make visible the structural violence underpinning American criminal justice. See, e.g., Michelle Brown, "Visual Criminology and Carceral Studies," *Theoretical Criminology* 18, no. 2 (2014): 176–97.

Epilogue: W(h)ither Crimesploitation?

1. Debra Seagal, "Tales from the Cutting Room Floor: The Reality of 'Reality-Based' Television," *Harper's Magazine* 287 (November 1993): 50–57, 56.

2. James Wolcott, "Car 54, Where Are You?" *New Yorker*, February 8, 1993, 104–5, 105.

3. Kim Moy, "EW Reality-TV Show Lets CHP Pursue Fame," *Sacramento Bee*, March 29, 1993.

4. Matt Furber, Audra D. S. Burch, and Frances Robles, "What Happened in the Chaotic Moments Before George Floyd Died," *New York Times*, May 29, 2020. The official time of death was listed as taking place about an hour after Floyd stopped responding while Chauvin held him down. It is unclear precisely when he died.

5. "TV Show Cops, Criticized for Glorifying Police Aggression, Cancelled after 32 Seasons," *The Guardian*, June 10, 2020, and Andrew Paul, "'Cops' TV Show Canceled as Police Propaganda Loses Shine after George Floyd," *NBC News Online*, June 10, 2020, https://www.nbcnews.com/think/opinion/cops-tv-show-canceled-amid-george-floyd-defund-police-about-ncna1229316.

6. Scott J. Croteau, "Chief Says 'Cops' Not Good for City; Television Show Pulls Up Stakes," *Worcester Telegram and Gazette*, July 28, 2006.

7. "Civil Rights Group Demands FOX Drop 'COPS,'" *New Pittsburgh Courier*, March 27, 2013.

8. According to San Diego mayor Todd Gloria, much of this funding is for nondiscretionary purposes, such as pension costs. Andrew Bowen, "Why Is San Diego's Mayor Adding $19 Million to the Police Budget?" *KPBS*, April 23, 2021, https://www.reuters.com/world/us/george-floyd-bill-misses-anniversary-deadline-us-lawmakers-say-prospects-are-2021-05-26/.

9. Wilborn P. Nobles III, "Crime Poses Crucial Test in Mayoral Race," *Atlanta Journal-Constitution*, July 20, 2021.

10. Trevor Hunnicutt and Susan Cornwell, "George Floyd Bill Misses Anniversary Deadline, but U.S. Lawmakers Say Prospects Are Good," *Reuters*, May 25, 2021, https://www.reuters.com/world/us/george-floyd-bill-misses-anniversary-deadline-us-lawmakers-say-prospects-are-2021-05-26/.

11. Megan Brenan, "Americans' Confidence in Major U.S. Institutions Dips," *Gallup News*, July 14, 2021, https://news.gallup.com/poll/352316/americans-confidence-major-institutions-dips.aspx.

12. And even the cancelation of *Cops* is somewhat misleading. The program was dumped by Paramount, but the production company quietly resumed filming episodes for overseas markets in the summer of 2020. Rick Porter, "'Cops' Quietly Resumes Production," *Hollywood Reporter*, October 1, 2020, https://www.hollywoodreporter.com/tv/tv-news/cops-quietly-resumes-production-4069865/.

13. Examples include *Narcoworld: Dope Stories* (2019), *Dope* (2019), *The Business of Drugs* (2020), *Drug Lords* (2018), *Inside the Real Narcos* (2019), and *Narcos: Mexico* (2020).

14. "It's Kill or Be Killed," episode 1 of *Narcoworld: Dope Stories*, executive produced by Jeremy Dear and Chris Lent, aired November 22, 2019 on Netflix, https://www.netflix.com/title/81169145.

15. Mike Vorhaus, "Expect Podcast Ad Revenue to Be Up in 2020: Study," *Forbes*, July 20, 2020, https://www.forbes.com/sites/mikevorhaus/2020/07/20/podcast-revenue-to-be-up-in-2020/?sh=7b99ce5416d0.

16. *Casefile*, https://casefilepodcast.com/; *Serial Killers*, narrated by Greg Polcyn and Vanessa Richardson, https://www.parcast.com/serial; *Black Girl Missing*, https://blackgirlmissingpod.com/; *The Generation Why*, narrated by Aaron and Justin, https://genwhypod.com/; *My Favorite Murder*, narrated by Karen Kilgariff and Georgia Hardstark, https://myfavoritemurder.com/; *Last Podcast on the Left*, narrated by Ben Kissel, Marcus Parks, and Henry Zebrowski, https://www.lastpodcastontheleft.com/.

17. Nicholas Quah, "The Best Podcasts of 2019," *Vulture*, December 5, 2019, retrieved from https://www.vulture.com/article/best-podcasts-2019.html. *Vulture*'s 2020 list includes several arguably crimesploitative podcasts, such as *Floodlines* (about the US government's bad response to Hurricane Katrina), *Reveal: American Rehab* (about capitalism and the drug rehab industry), and *Slow Burn: David Duke* (about KKK leader turned mainstream politician David Duke).

18. *In the Dark*, narrated by Madeleine Baran, https://features.apmreports.org/in-the-dark/.

19. On the way images of violence and suffering can settle and unsettle "regimes of representation," see Eamonn Carrabine, "Seeing Things: Violence, Voyeurism and the Camera," *Theoretical Criminology* 18, no. 2 (2014): 134–58.

Index

THE CULTURAL LIVES OF LAW
Austin Sarat, Editor

The Cultural Lives of Law series brings insights and approaches from cultural studies to law and tries to secure for law a place in cultural analysis. Books in the series focus on the production, interpretation, consumption, and circulation of legal meanings. They take up the challenges posed as boundaries collapse between as well as within cultures, and as the circulation of legal meanings becomes more fluid. They also attend to the ways law's power in cultural production is renewed and resisted.

Nesam McMillan, *Imagining the International: Crime, Justice, and the Promise of Community*
2020

Jeffrey R. Dudas, *Raised Right: Fatherhood in Modern American Conservatism*
2017

Renée Ann Cramer, *Pregnant with the Stars: Watching and Wanting the Celebrity Baby Bump*
2015

Sora Y. Han, *Letters of the Law: Race and the Fantasy of Colorblindness*
2015

Marianne Constable, *Our Word Is Our Bond: How Legal Speech Acts*
2014

Joshua C. Wilson, *The Street Politics of Abortion: Speech, Violence, and America's Culture Wars*
2013

Irus Braverman, *Zooland: The Institution of Captivity*
2012

Nora Gilbert, *Better Left Unsaid: Victorian Novels, Hays Code Films, and the Benefits of Censorship*
2012

Edited by Winnifred Fallers Sullivan, Robert A. Yelle, and Mateo Taussig-Rubbo, *After Secular Law*
2011

Keith J. Bybee, *All Judges Are Political—Except When They Are Not: Acceptable Hypocrisies and the Rule of Law*
2010

Susan Sage Heinzelman, *Riding the Black Ram: Law, Literature, and Gender*
2010

David M. Engel and Jaruwan S. Engel, *Tort, Custom, and Karma:
Globalization and Legal Consciousness in Thailand*
2010

Ruth A. Miller, *Law in Crisis: The Ecstatic Subject of Natural Disaster*
2009

Ravit Reichman, *The Affective Life of Law: Legal Modernism
and the Literary Imagination*
2009

Edited by David M. Engel and Michael McCann, *Fault Lines:
Tort Law as Cultural Practice*
2008

William P. MacNeil, *Lex Populi: The Jurisprudence of Popular Culture*
2007

Edited by Austin Sarat and Christian Boulanger, *The Cultural Lives
of Capital Punishment: Comparative Perspectives*

The authorized representative in the EU for product safety and compliance is:
Mare Nostrum Group
B.V Doelen 72
4831 GR Breda
The Netherlands

www.ingramcontent.com/pod-product-compliance
Lightning Source LLC
Chambersburg PA
CBHW030849270326
41928CB00008B/1284